Fearfully & Wonderfully Wired: God, the Brain, and Your Anxious Child

A Practical and Prayerful Companion for Parents of Anxious Children

By Kelly Whittaker for Erinnah Group Ltd

Fearfully & Wonderfully Wired: God, the Brain, and Your Anxious Child

Copyright © 2025 Erinnah Group Ltd and Kelly Whittaker
All rights reserved.

No part of this publication may be reproduced, stored in a retrieval system, or transmitted in any form or by any means—electronic, mechanical, photocopying, recording, scanning, or otherwise—without the prior written permission of the publisher and copyright holder, except as permitted by applicable copyright laws or expressly authorized in writing.

This book is sold subject to the condition that it shall not, by way of trade or otherwise, be lent, resold, hired out, or otherwise circulated in any format without the publisher's prior consent in any form of binding or cover other than that in which it is published and without a similar condition being imposed on the subsequent purchaser.

For permissions, inquiries, or bulk orders, please contact:
Erinnah Group Ltd www.erinnah.org

Printed in Australia

ISBN: 978-1-7642320-0-5

Thank you for purchasing this book, as all proceeds go towards our charitable mission. This book was written as part of the mission of Erinnah Group Ltd, a registered Australian charity dedicated to *advancing the emotional and spiritual wellbeing of children and families through a Christian lens.*

At the heart of our work is Erinnah's Treehouse — an innovative online program designed for children aged 6–12, where psychological science and biblical wisdom meet in a safe, engaging, and faith-filled environment. Through animated episodes, tools, and supportive content, the Treehouse helps kids learn to understand anxiety, develop healthy coping strategies, trust God in the midst of fear, worry, or sadness and build resilience — emotionally and spiritually.

This book was created for *you* — the parent, carer, or faith leader — to help you walk alongside children with confidence and compassion. You don't have to do this alone. Whether you're reading this book, listening to our podcast (*Erinnah's Treehouse Family*), or using our children's program — you're part of a growing community that believes that truth with tenderness, and growth with grace belong together.

To find out more, see our other resources, or access the children's Treehouse program, visit: www.erinnah.org

<u>Disclaimer</u>

This book is intended for educational and devotional purposes only. It is designed to offer general guidance, emotional support, and practical tools for parents navigating childhood anxiety from a Christian and psychological perspective.

It does not replace medical advice, psychological diagnosis, or professional treatment. Every child is unique, and anxiety can present in a range of ways. If you are concerned about your child's mental health, behaviour, or development, we strongly encourage you to consult with a qualified healthcare or mental health professional.

While every effort has been made to provide accurate and helpful information, the author and publisher disclaim any liability arising directly or indirectly from the use of this material.

If your child is in crisis or distress, please seek help immediately through your local mental health service or emergency provider.

The names used in this book are not real names identifying persons or cases, but are used to illustrate examples of the concepts taught in the book.

Contents

Introduction
How This Book Fits into Erinnah Group's Mission
How to Use This Book as a Parent
A Note on Seeking Professional Help

Chapter 1: Is This Just a Phase? Or Something More?

Discerning your child's emotional needs with grace and wisdom

Chapter 2: Wired Differently

Understanding the nervous system and the roots of anxious behaviour

Chapter 3: What's Really Going On?

Peeking beneath the surface of big reactions

Chapter 4: Feelings Have Names

Helping your child recognise, name, and process emotions

Chapter 5: From Avoidance to Approach

Building courage with biblical and psychological tools

Chapter 6: The Perfectionism Trap

Why some anxious kids try so hard to get it "just right"

Chapter 7: When the Body Feels It First

Somatic symptoms, interoception, and calming strategies that work

Chapter 8: When Letting Go Is the Bravest Thing

Surrendering control without surrendering care

Chapter 9: Preparing for the Real World

Helping your child step into school, social life, and independence

Chapter 10: When Life Doesn't Go to Plan

Supporting your child through disappointment and grief

Chapter 11: Planting Seeds for the Long Haul

Creating a family culture that nurtures emotional and spiritual resilience

There's a moment most parents won't admit out loud — the moment you find yourself staring at your child's tear-streaked face, your own jaw clenched, and thinking, *"I don't know how to help you."*

You've tried being calm. You've tried being firm. You've Googled. Prayed. Whispered encouragement through gritted teeth. But the meltdowns keep coming — over school drop-offs, itchy tags, loud hand dryers, unexpected changes, and sometimes... for no clear reason at all.

As a mental health clinician and a mother, I've sat on both sides of that moment. I've held the clipboard and the child. And I've learned that raising an anxious child takes more than good intentions and deep breaths. It takes compassion, understanding, practical tools — and faith that anchors you both.

This book is here to offer all three.

I came to see that parenting an anxious child is holy ground. It's sacred work — not because we're always doing it well, but because God meets us in it. In the mess. In the fears. In the late-night whispers. In the moments we whisper back, "Lord, I don't know what to do." This book was born in those moments.

It's for every parent who has:

- Googled "is this normal?"

- Tried deep breathing while their child sobbed under the dining table

- Cried after the bedtime battle ended in slammed doors and soft guilt

- Wondered if anxiety meant their child was broken (or if they were)

Let me reassure you now: you're not broken. And neither is your child. You're both beautifully human. And deeply loved by a God who knows all about fear — and who tells us over and over again not to face it alone.

What This Book Is (and Isn't)

This book isn't a textbook. And it's not a lecture. It's part toolbox, part devotional, part "grab a cuppa and let's talk about it." It's a gentle companion through the ups and downs of parenting anxious kids — filled with:

- Psychological strategies that really work

- Biblical wisdom that restores perspective

- Honest reflections from the frontlines of parenting

- Prayers to guide your words, your reactions, and your heart

Each chapter blends insight with grace. It ends not just with tips, but with a pause — a chance to breathe, reflect, and reset with God. Because when you're raising a child who feels everything deeply, you need more than just a plan. You need hope. And you need a reminder that you're not walking this road alone. So welcome. To this book. To the Treehouse — a place where kids and grown-ups can both learn how to feel, to pray, and to heal.

Chapter 1

Is This Just a Phase? Or Something More?

Discerning your child's emotional needs with grace and wisdom

---

It was a regular Monday morning. We were running late for school, and I was trying to stay calm while spreading peanut butter on toast with one hand and locating a missing library book with the other. That's when I heard it: the sound of quiet defiance from the hallway. My daughter had stopped getting dressed. She stood still, arms crossed, her little brow furrowed with determination. "I'm not wearing those socks. They feel *wrong*."

I glanced down. They were the same socks she'd worn a hundred times — plain white cotton, no holes, no rough seams. We didn't have time for a wardrobe negotiation. I gently encouraged. She refused. I insisted. She cried. It was only socks… but it felt like something more. At first, I chalked it up to a "Monday morning mood." But the meltdowns kept coming.

Different triggers, same intensity. And I started to wonder:

Is this just a phase... or is something deeper going on?

Children experiencing anxiety may not say, "I feel anxious." Instead, they ask questions that seem silly or frustrating... or they melt down altogether.

You might hear:

- "What if I get sick?"

- "What if the toilet floods again?"

- "What if my teacher yells at me?"

- "What if you die?"

These questions don't come from defiance — they come from a brain that feels unsure and a nervous system that's scanning for danger. In psychological terms, this is called hypervigilance — and it's common in anxious children, even if they seem fine most of the day. It can show up around:

- Age 4–6, when the imagination blooms and separation anxiety may spike

- Starting school, when performance and routine fears surface

- After a big life change, like a move, illness, or family stress

- At bedtime, when stillness invites all the swirling thoughts in

Understanding anxiety with science in one hand and Scripture in the other.

When a child feels anxious, their brain isn't being "bad." It's being protective. And honestly, that's something we can respect. The part of the brain most active in anxiety is called the amygdala — the brain's smoke alarm. Its job is to detect threat and launch the body into action: fight, flight, freeze, or fawn. This alarm system is fast, automatic, and emotionally charged — because it's designed to keep us alive. The problem is, in anxious children, the smoke alarm often goes off when there's no real fire.

Maybe it's a new teacher. A buzzing bee. A looming speech at assembly. Even the thought of disappointment or unfamiliarity can spark alarm. And when the amygdala is firing, the thinking brain — the prefrontal cortex — temporarily shuts down.

That's why:

- Your child can't "just calm down" on command
- They might forget things they usually know
- Reasoning, bribing, or logic often don't work in the moment

It's not that they *won't* listen — it's that they *can't* right now. Their body is flooded with stress hormones (like cortisol and adrenaline), and their brain is yelling, "*Danger!*" Here's the beautiful overlap: God is the designer of the brain. God knows this wiring and we can take comfort in that. He knows how fear affects us — and how much we need safe, calm presence in those moments.

"Fear not, for I have redeemed you; I have called you by name, you are mine." — Isaiah 43:1

God's first response to fear is not correction. It's connection. He meets His people with, "Do not be afraid," not "Get over it." As parents, we reflect His nature when we offer our children co-regulation — staying calm and steady, so their nervous system can borrow ours.

> *"He will quiet you with his love."* – *Zephaniah 3:17*

Our love can't rewire the brain overnight, but it can build new pathways over time. Every moment we respond with warmth instead of panic, we help their brain learn: *"I can feel this… and be okay."*

Bridging Clinical Insight and Faith

Christian parents can trust both the science of the mind and the wisdom of God. There's a quiet fear many Christian parents carry: "If I rely on psychology… am I sidelining my faith?" Or the reverse: "If I only rely on prayer, am I failing to get my child the help they need?" I want to gently say: You don't have to choose. Psychology and Scripture are not enemies. They are friends in the healing work of raising children with wisdom and compassion.

Clinical psychology gives us tools — Tools for understanding brain function, behaviour, and patterns of emotion. Tools for noticing what's normal and what might need extra support. Tools for building resilience, calming the body, and developing coping skills. It offers evidence-based practices grounded in research — not to replace prayer or faith, but to work alongside them. Think of it like this: If your child breaks their arm, you pray. You also get an X-ray. If your child's emotional world is out of alignment, you pray. You can also reach for proven strategies and support. This isn't lack of faith — it's faithful stewardship.

Scripture gives us meaning, identity, comfort, and eternal truth. It reminds us that we are not defined by our fears — we are God's beloved. It reframes suffering in light of God's sovereignty and grace. It teaches us not just *what to do*, but *who to trust*. Where psychology can explain how anxiety works, Scripture speaks to the why — the deeper narrative that grounds us when storms hit.

> *"Do not be anxious about anything, but in everything, by prayer and petition, with thanksgiving, present your requests to God."* – Philippians 4:6

This verse is often misunderstood as a command to simply stop feeling anxious. But in the context of neuroscience, it takes on a richer meaning. Prayer is *not* the opposite of anxiety. Prayer is the pathway out of it — it's co-regulation with God. Just like a parent's calm presence helps a child regulate, *God's presence helps us restore peace to our minds.*

Integration in Action

So what does this look like in daily life?

- When your child is panicking, you don't just quote Scripture *at* them — you breathe with them, kneel beside them, and whisper truth into their storm.

- When your child avoids school, you don't dismiss it with "just have more faith." You ask curious questions, use exposure techniques, and pray together for courage.

- When your child is locked in a perfectionism spiral, you affirm their worth in God's eyes, and offer cognitive behavioural tools to challenge all-or-nothing thinking.

This is integration. This is faith-informed psychology and psychologically sound faith. It is not weak. It is not worldly. It's the model of Jesus, who saw the person's pain *and* the person's potential. Who touched eyes and hearts. Who said both "Be healed" and "Do not be afraid."

If you've ever felt caught between worlds — between prayer and practice, devotion and diagnosis — know this: God is the author of both. He is the God of your child's brain, and the lover of their soul. He provides wisdom through Scripture *and* through professionals He has equipped. You are not failing when you seek help. You are walking faithfully — with both hands open.

> *"For the Lord gives wisdom; from his mouth come knowledge and understanding."* – Proverbs 2:6

PSYCH INSIGHT:

Anxiety can be managed through practices like exposure therapy, deep breathing, and cognitive reframing — all of which are shown to help retrain the brain and reduce emotional overreactions.

FAITH PARALLEL:

Scripture teaches emotional regulation, too: "Be still and know that I am God" (Psalm 46:10) and "Take every thought captive" (2 Corinthians 10:5) are spiritual truths that mirror what science confirms.

Together they teach us:

God wired our brains for healing, and invites us to participate in that renewal — spiritually, emotionally, and relationally.

So when your child's anxiety feels big — like it's swallowing the whole day — take a breath. You're not a failure. You're raising a child with a very alert alarm

system. And God?   He sees that system. He knows their frame.   He holds their every "What if…"
And He gently speaks the "Even if…" that brings peace.

> *"Even if I walk through the valley of the shadow of death, I will fear no evil, for you are with me."* — Psalm 23:4

"The Anxious Brain vs. The Comforted Brain"

Anxious Brain	Comforted Brain
Amygdala lit up	Calmer brain circuits
Prefrontal cortex offline	Thinking brain online
Body flooded with cortisol	Nervous system soothed
Child can't "think straight"	Child feels seen and supported

"A calm adult helps turn off the child's alarm."

A Quick Discernment Framework for Parents

If you're wondering whether what you're seeing is *just a phase* or something that needs support, here are three questions I ask as a clinician — and a parent:

1. **Is it affecting everyday life?**
    (Are they avoiding things they used to enjoy? Struggling to cope daily?)

2. **Is it getting worse, not better, over time?**
    (Some things resolve naturally; others escalate if unaddressed.)

3. **Is it interfering with their relationships?**
    (Are friendships, learning, or parent-child connections strained?)

If the answer is "yes" to one or more — don't panic. You're not diagnosing. You're *discerning.* You're opening the door to curiosity, compassion, and maybe seeking wise support.

I'll never forget one morning before school when my daughter sat on the floor, socks in hand, tears running down her cheeks. She insisted they felt "too crunchy." I checked. Nothing unusual. I suggested different ones. No luck. Eventually, with time running out, I raised my voice, told her we had to go, and hustled her into the car — both of us frustrated and fragile. It wasn't until later — after a few repeat episodes — that I realised it wasn't the socks. It was anxiety.

The unfamiliar pressure of a school day. The fear of forgetting something. The helpless feeling she couldn't quite name. I hadn't failed. But I *had* missed a moment of insight.   And that's okay. Parenting isn't about perfection — it's about growing in wisdom, circling back with compassion, and remembering that grace covers both our children and us.

Some behaviours *are* just phases. Children might: Suddenly become picky eaters, get clingy after holidays, develop a weird obsession with bandaids, or pretend to be puppies for three straight weeks. These moments don't always need intervention — just patience and a sense of humour. What matters is how you observe patterns, and whether you feel concerned or confused by what's happening over time. When in doubt? You don't have to figure it out alone.

▲ Reflection & Prayer

Reflect:

- When have I brushed something off as "just a phase" that might have been a cry for help?

- Have I been more focused on fixing behaviour than understanding what's behind it?

- How does God want to shape me into a parent who listens with the heart?

Pray:

God, give me ears to hear what my child isn't saying out loud.
Give me eyes to see beneath the behaviour.
Give me wisdom to know when to wait, and when to act.
And give me peace, even when I don't have the full picture.
You love them even more than I do. I trust you with their heart.

When your child starts refusing to go to school, worries about their socks "feeling weird," or bursts into tears over forgotten library day, your brain goes into detective mode. You wonder: "Is this normal?" "Are they just sensitive?" "Did I do something wrong?" "Should I wait it out… or do something?" Maybe a well-meaning friend shrugs and says, *"Kids are just like*

that." Or your own internal dialogue says, *"Don't overreact. They'll grow out of it."* And yes — children *do* go through phases. They regress, leap forward, get emotional before a growth spurt, have weird attachment to obscure socks or sandwich crust rules. That's part of their job as kids. But sometimes, what looks like a quirky phase is actually your child's way of saying: *"I'm overwhelmed." "I'm scared."*
"I need help but don't know how to ask."

In the thick of parenting, it's easy to become behaviour-focused. We look at tantrums, refusals, clinginess — and we react. We want it solved. Sorted. Settled before we've had our second cup of tea. But Scripture invites us to go deeper. God doesn't parent us based on symptoms — He cares about the state of the heart. And He calls us to do the same with our children.

> *"The purposes of a person's heart are deep waters, but one who has insight draws them out."* — Proverbs 20:5

Children are not simple just because they are small. They have real fears, real longings, real needs — and often, very few words to express them. Jesus never dismissed children as silly or dramatic. He welcomed them. He *blessed* them. He made space for them in a world that often wanted them pushed to the side.

When we slow down to look beneath the behaviour, we become like Jesus — *making room.*

Room for emotion. Room for vulnerability. Room for trust to grow. In today's world, there's pressure to parent like a manager: Stay on schedule. Minimise disruptions. Keep the system running smoothly. But Jesus invites us to parent like a shepherd.

> *"He gathers the lambs in his arms and carries them close to his heart; he gently leads those that have young."* — Isaiah 40:11

That verse speaks to us as much as it speaks about our kids. He doesn't rush us. He leads us *gently* — even when we don't get it right the first time. If we want to help our children navigate anxiety and big feelings, it starts by seeing them the way God does: as image-bearers, not inconveniences, as whole humans, not behavioural problems, as hearts in formation — not yet fully grown, but deeply loved. When we begin from that place, we're more patient. More curious. Less reactive. And far more likely to reflect the kind of parenting our children will carry with them into their own faith journey.

Parent Reflection:

When I think about my child's heart, do I tend to focus more on behaviour or on what might be going on beneath it?

What would it look like today to pause, connect, and draw out the "deep waters" instead of trying to fix the surface waves?

What Psychology Says About Early Signs of Anxiety

"I always thought anxiety looked like panic attacks. I didn't realise my daughter's clinginess and tummy aches were her way of crying out." — Emma, mum of 2.

Here's something every parent should know: Anxiety is not always loud. Sometimes it looks like:

- Constant reassurance-seeking ("Will you be there?" "Are you sure?" "What if…?")
- Irritability or outbursts over small things
- Trouble sleeping or excessive tiredness

- Avoidance (not wanting to go to school, birthday parties, new activities)

- Tummy aches and headaches with no medical cause

- Perfectionism or fear of making mistakes

- Meltdowns that seem to come "out of nowhere"

Children don't always say *"I'm anxious."* Instead, they show us in behaviour, mood, body symptoms — or even in what they *refuse* to do. This is where faith and psychology meet beautifully. Science helps us recognise the signs. God helps us respond with peace, patience, and prayer — instead of fear. "Behaviour is the signal, not the story."

I once worked with a child — we'll call her Sophie — who clung to her mum's arm every morning at drop-off, crying as if she were being abandoned in the desert. Her mum was exhausted, confused, and a little embarrassed. Everyone told her it was just a phase. "Don't coddle her. She'll stop eventually." But deep down, she knew something else was going on. After a few conversations, some play-based therapy, and a lot of gentleness, we uncovered that Sophie wasn't just "clingy." She had overheard a news story that frightened her, and believed something bad would happen to Mum if they were apart. It wasn't just a phase. It was anxiety. And it needed kindness, not criticism.

Discernment Over Diagnosis

As a clinician and a Christian, I believe in labels *when they help.* But I believe more in discernment — that Spirit-led, heart-attuned ability to ask:

- What's underneath this behaviour?
- What's my child afraid of?
- How can I offer safety and truth right now?

Sometimes a phase is a phase. Sometimes it's a cry for help. Either way, we don't walk blindly — we ask God for wisdom.

> *"If any of you lacks wisdom, let him ask of God, who gives generously..."* – James 1:5

Here are three quick tools to begin discerning your child's big feelings:

1. **Keep a simple "worry journal"**

- Note when big emotions happen: time, situation, physical symptoms
- Patterns often reveal what's anxiety-driven

2. **Ask open-ended questions**

    - Try "What part felt tricky today?" or "If your feelings could talk, what would they say?"

3. **Don't rush the reassurance**

    - Instead of "You're fine," try "That does sound scary. Let's figure it out together."
    - Connection first, correction or logic later

Reflection & Prayer

Reflection Prompt:
What situations make me question whether it's a phase or something deeper?
Have I been brushing things off… or catastrophising?
What is God prompting me to look at with new eyes?

Prayer:
Lord, you see the heart of my child more clearly than I ever could. Help me to see beneath the surface. Give me insight when I feel unsure. Help me to respond with curiosity instead of fear. And let my presence reflect your steady, compassionate love.
Amen.

Word over you, dear parent.
As you parent through uncertainty, may you feel the nearness of the God who sees both your child's heart and yours. May His wisdom lead you, His peace guard you, and His joy return to your home.

In the next chapter, we'll unpack where anxiety actually comes from — and why your child's response isn't defiance, but design.

Chapter 2

Where Does Anxiety Come From?

Understanding the roots so we can grow something new

Some children don't just *feel* more — they feel everything more. The noise of a hand dryer in a public toilet. The change in tone when a parent is slightly stressed. The tightness of socks, the flicker of lights, the idea that a classmate is upset. These children notice things that others breeze past. And when they do, their whole body can react. This isn't manipulation. It's not attention-seeking. It's not a result of bad parenting. It's their nervous system doing its job — just a little louder than usual.

Nervous System 101 (The Gentle Version)

At the core of our emotional experience is something called the autonomic nervous system. It has two main settings:

- Sympathetic system — gets us ready to "fight, flight, or freeze"

- Parasympathetic system — helps us rest, digest, and feel safe

Children with sensitive wiring tend to have quicker "on-switches" in their sympathetic system. Their bodies go into alert mode faster, and it takes longer for them to come back down. Their threshold for stimulation is lower. Their tolerance for uncertainty is narrower. But their capacity for deep connection, creativity, and spiritual insight is often much greater. This is not dysfunction. This is a different setting — like having the volume turned up on life.

In everyday life, a child with a more sensitive nervous system might:

- Be easily startled or distressed by loud sounds or busy places

- Avoid new situations unless slowly introduced

- Have "big" feelings that rise fast and crash hard

- Overthink or over-prepare for simple things (like packing their schoolbag or choosing a snack)

- Seek reassurance — not because they're needy, but because their body craves felt safety

God made some children with fire in their belly, others with softness in their spirit. Some are bold. Others are thoughtful. Some lead. Others sense what others can't articulate.

> *"He will not crush the weakest reed or put out a flickering candle." – Isaiah 42:3 (NLT)*

God doesn't overlook the sensitive child — He defends them. He doesn't rush them — He meets them in the still, quiet places.

🧠 NEURO INSIGHT:

Sensitive children may live more often in "fight or flight" mode, even if they seem calm on the outside. This affects sleep, digestion, memory, and mood.

💬 FAITH PARALLEL:

"Come to me, all who are weary and burdened, and I will give you rest." (Matthew 11:28)
Jesus offers what the body and soul both crave — rest. His presence is a balm for the overstimulated child.

If this sounds like your child, your parenting may need to include:

- More preparation for transitions
- More sensory awareness (e.g., textures, noise, light)
- More patience with processing time

- More grace when others say "they'll grow out of it" and you know they just need support

The world may label them as too intense, too emotional, too fragile. But God sees them as tenderhearted, deeply attuned, and worth pursuing. Your calm presence is the soil they'll grow confidence in. And their nervous system — while sensitive — is also *trainable*. With safety, support, and time, their brains can learn that not every beep, bump, or change means danger. You're not just raising a "sensitive kid."
You're raising a future artist, advocate, shepherd, or listener who was *made* for connection.

Let's break it down into three core contributors:

1. Biology (The Temperament They Were Born With).

Luca had always been "a bit on edge." As a baby, he startled easily. As a toddler, he hated loud hand dryers. Now, at age seven, his parents noticed he didn't cope well with surprise changes. If they turned left instead of right on the school run, he'd panic. If his teacher raised her voice to someone else, he'd shrink into himself for the rest of the day.

One time, his mum asked him to pick a treat from the bakery. He stood frozen, staring at the options. Then he burst into tears. Too many choices. Too much pressure.

Luca's nervous system ran hot all the time. His fight-or-flight mode flicked on at the slightest whiff of unpredictability. But what made him anxious also made him deeply aware — of how others felt, of when someone was hurting, and of when quiet was more sacred than noise. His sensitivity wasn't a flaw. It was his superpower. But he needed a parent who saw it that way too.

Parent Prompt:
Can you think of a time your child reacted "too much" — and it might've been their sensitive wiring, not disobedience?

Some kids are born with more sensitive nervous systems. They notice more. Feel more. Worry more. You'll hear terms like: Highly sensitive, Slow to warm up, Reactive, Cautious or Risk-Averse. This isn't a flaw — it's just wiring. And research shows that these children often become deeply empathetic, thoughtful, and spiritually attuned adults when nurtured well.

> *"For you created my inmost being; you knit me together in my mother's womb."* – Psalm 139:13

God isn't surprised by your child's sensitivity. He designed it with purpose.

2. Experience (What They've Been Through)

When Ava was four, she was hospitalised for a sudden stomach bug that wouldn't stop. She vomited so often and violently that she had to stay overnight for fluids. It was traumatic — the pokes, the machines, the smell of antiseptic, and the way the lights never really went out in the emergency room.

Now, three years later, she still doesn't sleep well. She worries that if she eats something "weird," she'll throw up again. She washes her hands obsessively and sniffs food before tasting it. Her parents didn't immediately connect it to that hospital stay — it seemed like so long ago — until one night she whispered, "What if I throw up in my sleep like before?" The fear was no longer in her belly — it was in her memory. Ava wasn't being difficult or fussy. Her body had remembered what her words couldn't yet express.

And her parents' gentle reassurance, over time, helped her feel safe again at night — and safe with food, too.

Parent Prompt:
Was there a moment in your child's early years that may have left a bigger emotional imprint than you realised?

Even in safe homes, children may go through changes that increase anxiety, like starting school, medical issues, moving house, family stress (even unspoken). Sometimes anxiety comes from trauma, yes — but more often, it grows from accumulated stress that overwhelms their developing coping system. What feels small to us can feel enormous to a child. And they may not have words to explain it. This is why we lead with curiosity, not correction. We're not trying to interrogate the cause — we're trying to create safety around it.

3. Meaning (What They Believe About Their World)

The third layer is one we often overlook: What story is my child telling themselves?

Maybe:

- "If I get it wrong, I'll get in trouble."

- "If Mum's not near me, something bad will happen."

- "If people laugh, they're laughing at me."

- "If I feel scared, it means I'm not okay."

These stories aren't always taught directly. Sometimes they're absorbed through moments of fear, perfectionism, or feeling out of control. And they shape how our child interacts with the world — and with God. Emily was the kind of child who always coloured inside the lines. She loved gold stars and being called "clever." Her parents praised her often — not realising that every "Well done!" reinforced a belief forming quietly in her heart: *If I get things wrong, I'm not lovable.*

At school, she started hiding incomplete work. At home, she'd melt down if a drawing didn't turn out exactly as she imagined. One day, when she accidentally spilled juice on her homework, she dissolved into sobs, saying, "I'm so stupid. My teacher won't like me anymore." Her parents were shocked. They'd never said anything like that. But children absorb beliefs like sponges — not just from what is said, but from what is celebrated, emphasised, or feared. It took time, but Emily's parents began praising effort more than outcome. They started saying things like, "I love you because you're you, not because of what you do." Slowly, the inner story changed.

Parent Prompt:

What messages might your child be absorbing — not just from your words, but from what you praise, correct, or worry about?

The Bible is filled with people who battled anxiety — often when they were young or called into unfamiliar territory:

- Moses trembled at the thought of public speaking.

- Jeremiah said, "I am only a child."

- Timothy needed repeated encouragement to stand firm.

- Even Jesus in Gethsemane cried out in distress before the cross.

And yet, God responded to each one with presence, not punishment.

"Fear not, for I am with you." – Isaiah 41:10

This isn't a command to suppress emotion. It's an invitation into connection. When we understand where anxiety comes from, we stop trying to squash it — and start walking with our children through it.

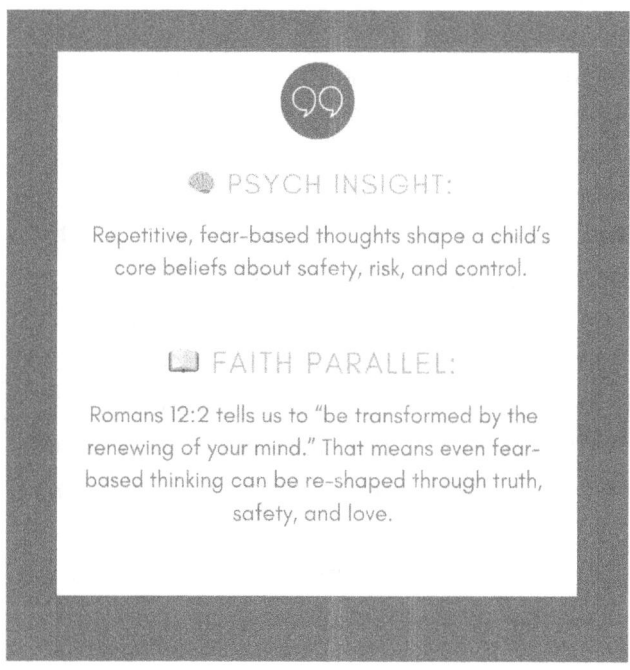

> **PSYCH INSIGHT:**
> Repetitive, fear-based thoughts shape a child's core beliefs about safety, risk, and control.
>
> **FAITH PARALLEL:**
> Romans 12:2 tells us to "be transformed by the renewing of your mind." That means even fear-based thinking can be re-shaped through truth, safety, and love.

If your child is anxious, it doesn't mean you've done something wrong. It means their brain is alert, their body is sensitive, and their spirit is asking for help. Your role isn't to make the anxiety disappear — it's to:

- Understand where it comes from

- Speak God's truth into it

- Offer co-regulation when it flares up

- Model what it looks like to feel fear... and still move forward

Because that's what courage is. And our children learn courage in the presence of calm, trusted love. You might be tempted right now to look back — to wonder if you missed signs, mishandled moments, or accidentally passed on your own anxiety. Let me stop you right there, gently. There is grace for what you didn't know. There is grace for what you're still learning. And there is grace for your child, whose brain may shout louder than you'd like — but whose life is held by a God who whispers peace.

Reflection & Prayer

Reflect:

- Have I been blaming myself or my child for their anxiety?

- Which of the three roots (biology, experience, meaning) seems most present right now?

- How can I show compassion — instead of frustration — in our next hard moment?

Pray:
Lord, thank You for the way You designed my child.
Thank You for making their heart tender and their thoughts rich, even when it overwhelms them.
Help me lead them with wisdom — not fear.
Help me guide them with insight — not guilt.
You are the safest place we could ever run.
Amen.

A Word Over You, Dear Parent

As you begin to understand where anxiety comes from — the sensitive wiring, the remembered moments, the hidden meanings — may you feel the pressure lift. You are not behind. You are not alone. You are not the reason for every fear. You are the steady guide your child needs, chosen by God for this season, for this soul.

May you find peace in knowing that your child's struggles are not the end of the story — they're the soil where trust can grow. May you stop blaming yourself for what you didn't know — and start walking forward with grace for what you're learning now. May your heart be filled not with fear, but with quiet courage: the kind that doesn't have all the answers, but knows the One who does. You are not raising a problem to be fixed.

You are raising a person to be loved. And God sees both of you — completely, tenderly, and without shame. He's not asking you to be perfect. He's asking you to stay close.

Chapter 3

What Anxiety Looks Like (When It Doesn't Look Like Anxiety)

Spotting hidden signs, soft signals, and big behaviour that's really a cry for safety

---

Chapter Purpose

This chapter will explore:

- Why anxiety often shows up as something else: defiance, perfectionism, clinginess, meltdowns

- Why "quiet" kids can still be anxious (internalising vs externalising anxiety)

- Examples of anxiety in everyday behaviour — including surprising ones

- The importance of compassionate interpretation before correction

- Encouragement for parents to observe, not just react

One child won't let you leave their room at bedtime. Another throws their lunchbox across the room after school. A third says nothing, but chews their shirt collar until it's soaked. Which one is anxious?

Possibly all of them. Anxiety doesn't always come knocking in the way we expect. It doesn't always look like shaking hands or tearful confessions. In fact, it rarely looks the way we imagine it — especially in children. Often, anxiety wears disguises. Sometimes it looks loud — like yelling or refusal. Sometimes it looks quiet — like silence or stomachaches. Sometimes it looks rebellious — but really, it's fear in costume. The problem is, we tend to respond to the *behaviour* without realising it's the doorbell to something deeper. Behind it? A heart that's unsure. A body that feels unsafe. A brain that's scanning the environment asking, *"Am I okay?"*

Our job isn't to guess every emotion perfectly. Our job is to knock gently on that door, and say, "I see something's going on. I'm here."

> *"People look at the outward appearance, but the Lord looks at the heart." – 1 Samuel 16:7*

Children don't often say, "Mum, I'm experiencing internalised fear rooted in a dysregulated nervous system." (Although wouldn't that make things easier?). Instead, they act it out. Or hold it in. Or melt down. Or freeze. Here are six of the most common — and often misunderstood — ways anxiety shows up in kids:

1. Clinginess

"Please don't go." -   A child who seems overly attached, who won't go into the classroom without you, or insists on sitting within arm's reach during dinner — may not be "needy." They may be experiencing separation anxiety or a deep need for safety that hasn't been met elsewhere.

PSYCH INSIGHT:

When a child is in fight-or-flight, they look for a safe base. That's you.

FAITH PARALLEL:

"Under His wings you will find refuge." (Psalm 91:4). Children mirror this instinct in seeking our closeness.

2. Defiance

"No! I'm not doing it!" - This is one of the trickiest presentations of anxiety — because it looks like willful disobedience. But often, children act out when a task feels overwhelming or unsafe (socially, emotionally, or cognitively).

Looks like: Refusing to go to school, throwing their shoes instead of putting them on, or arguing when asked to join a group activity.

Parent Reframe: What looks like rebellion might be anxiety's armour. The child pushes away the task — or you — to avoid the rising discomfort

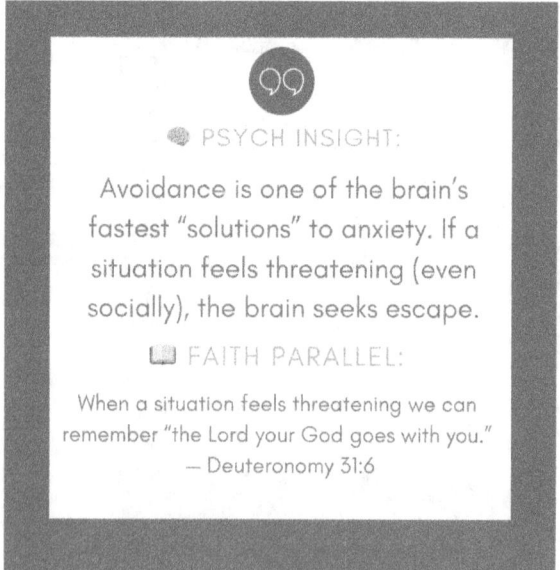

PSYCH INSIGHT:

Avoidance is one of the brain's fastest "solutions" to anxiety. If a situation feels threatening (even socially), the brain seeks escape.

FAITH PARALLEL:

When a situation feels threatening we can remember "the Lord your God goes with you."
— Deuteronomy 31:6

3. Perfectionism

"It's not right — I have to start over."

This child isn't just trying to do well — they're terrified of getting it wrong. Anxiety can latch onto performance, making even fun tasks feel loaded.

You might see: repeating tasks again and again, avoiding things they're unsure about, crumpling artwork in frustration, melting down when a mistake is made.

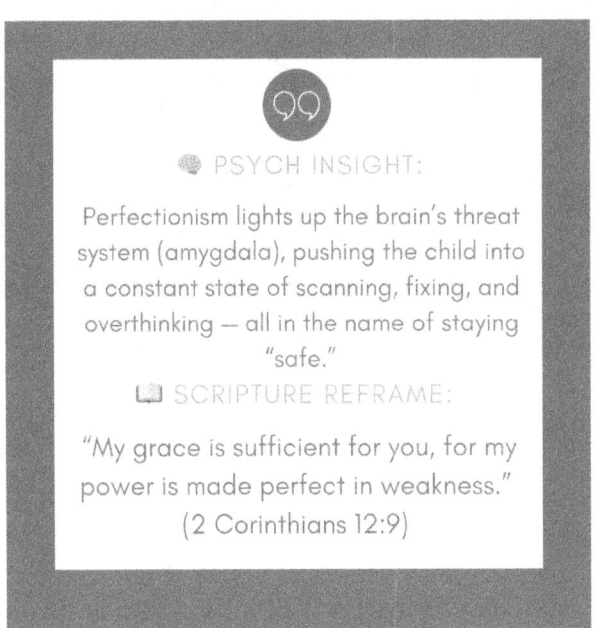

🧠 PSYCH INSIGHT:

Perfectionism lights up the brain's threat system (amygdala), pushing the child into a constant state of scanning, fixing, and overthinking — all in the name of staying "safe."

📖 SCRIPTURE REFRAME:

"My grace is sufficient for you, for my power is made perfect in weakness."
(2 Corinthians 12:9)

Our kids need to hear that failure isn't final — and love doesn't depend on outcomes.

4. Meltdowns

"Everything is too much." - Sometimes anxiety builds up slowly — like pressure in a balloon — until one small poke pops it. A meltdown over the wrong coloured plate, or being asked to brush their teeth, might actually be the release valve after a full day of silent tension. This is especially true for kids who mask their emotions in public and let it all out once they're home.

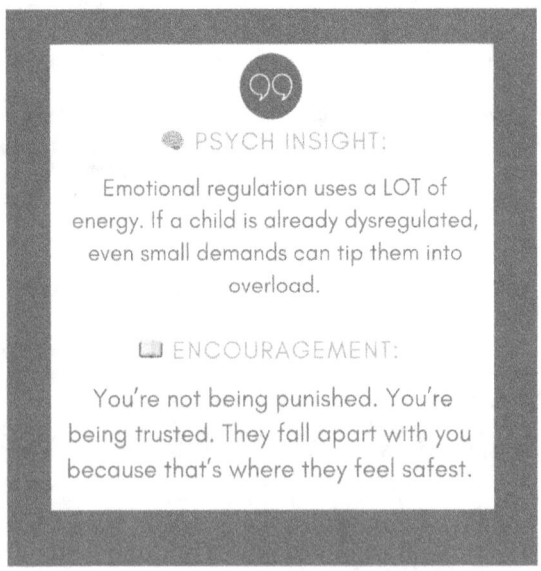

🧠 PSYCH INSIGHT:

Emotional regulation uses a LOT of energy. If a child is already dysregulated, even small demands can tip them into overload.

💬 ENCOURAGEMENT:

You're not being punished. You're being trusted. They fall apart with you because that's where they feel safest.

5. Avoidance

"I don't want to go." - Avoidance is anxiety's favourite trick. If something feels scary — even just slightly uncomfortable — the brain whispers, *"Just don't do it."* This might look like: refusing to try new food, not wanting to attend birthday parties, complaining of stomachaches before school, or withdrawing from activities they once enjoyed.

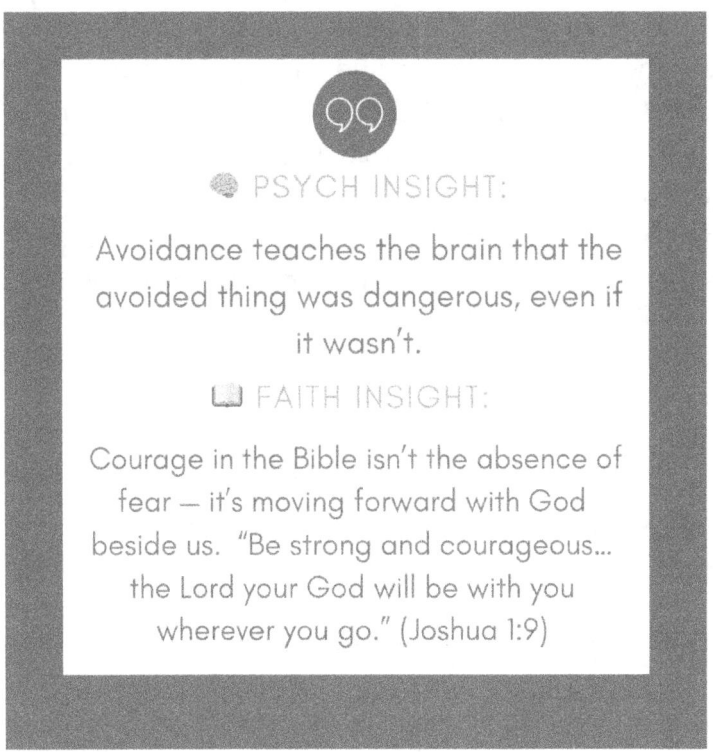

PSYCH INSIGHT:

Avoidance teaches the brain that the avoided thing was dangerous, even if it wasn't.

FAITH INSIGHT:

Courage in the Bible isn't the absence of fear — it's moving forward with God beside us. "Be strong and courageous... the Lord your God will be with you wherever you go." (Joshua 1:9)

Avoidance relieves anxiety temporarily — but it reinforces the fear long term.

Here's the trap: avoidance actually works — at least in the short term. When your child avoids the school play, the swim class, or trying something new, their anxiety drops instantly. They feel safe again. Relieved. In control. But this sends a powerful message to the brain: "Good thing we avoided that — it really must've been dangerous." And so the fear quietly grows. Each time the anxiety is avoided instead of faced with gentle support, it gets stronger. The child becomes more afraid next time, and less confident in their ability to cope. This creates what's known in psychology as the Cycle of Anxiety — a loop that reinforces fear, even when the original threat was never real.

Parent Prompt:

Can you think of something your child has been avoiding — and how you've responded to that avoidance?

What's one small, supported step they might be able to take next time… with you by their side?

Cycle of Anxiety

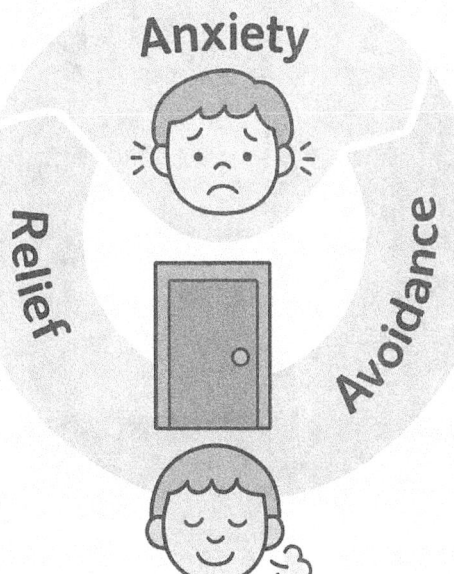

✝ Faith + 🧠 Brain NOTES

Avoiding anxiety brings short-term comfort, but teaches our brains to be afraid long-term.

But God promises, *"Fear does not control you."*
isaiah 41:10

PSYCH INSIGHT:

When we help our kids face their fears with small steps and safe presence, we don't just teach bravery — we help their brains rewire for peace.

FAITH INSIGHT:

Avoidance is a quick fix — but God calls us to long-term freedom. "Fear does not control you." (Isaiah 41:10)

6. Physical Symptoms

"My tummy hurts again."

For many children, anxiety doesn't show up emotionally — it shows up *physically.* Headaches, stomachaches, nausea, trouble sleeping, fidgeting or restlessness. Their nervous system is on high alert, and their body becomes the messenger.

> 💬 **PSYCH INSIGHT:**
> If your child frequently complains of vague or shifting physical symptoms, especially around stressful events — anxiety could be the root.
>
> 📖 **FAITH INSIGHT:**
> Jesus saw the whole person. He didn't separate the physical from the emotional or spiritual. "Daughter, your faith has healed you. Go in peace and be freed from your suffering." (Mark 5:34)

What's the Theme? Across all of these presentations, one truth echoes: The behaviour is not the problem. It's the signal. Our children are doing their best to cope with an internal alarm they don't yet know how to name. And that's where we come in — not as judges of behaviour, but as interpreters of it.

"The purposes of a person's heart are deep waters, but one who has insight draws them out." (Proverbs 20:5)

Two Kinds of Kids: Internalisers and Externalisers

Anxious kids don't all look the same. Some cry. Some yell. Some… just smile and say they're fine. As a mental health clinician, one of the most helpful distinctions I teach parents is this: There are two broad ways children tend to express anxiety:

- **Internalisers** turn it inward

- **Externalisers** turn it outward

Neither is right or wrong — just different expressions of the same overwhelmed nervous system.

Internalisers

These kids might:

- Withdraw when anxious

- Complain of vague physical symptoms

- Avoid situations quietly

- Try to stay "perfect" to avoid attention

- Cry quietly, daydream, or hold it all in

They're often praised for being easy, polite, or "good" — which can cause their anxiety to go unnoticed for a long time. They carry their fear like a weight in their pocket — heavy, but hidden.

Externalisers

These kids might:

- Yell or lash out when anxious

- Get angry or "refuse" to do things

- Become hyperactive or oppositional

- Create chaos when their world feels out of control

They're often misunderstood as "badly behaved" — when really, they're overwhelmed. They carry their fear like a balloon filled too full — one more poke and it pops.

Understanding which type your child leans toward helps you respond more wisely.

- Internalisers need gentle drawing out: "I've noticed you've been quiet. Want to tell me what's going on?"

- Externalisers need calm anchoring: "I can see this feels really big right now. I'm here. Let's get through it together."

Jesus met both types with the same approach: compassion first. The woman who wept at His feet… the child who threw themselves to the ground in distress… both were seen. Both were loved. Both were healed. Let's look at a few examples from real-life families (fictionalised and composite for privacy) where anxiety showed up in disguise — and how understanding the true cause changed everything.

Sam's Sunday Meltdowns

Every Sunday morning, 8-year-old Sam seemed to lose it. He'd refuse to get dressed, cry about itchy socks, throw his cereal. His parents thought he just didn't want to go to church.

Turns out, he *did* want to go — but he also dreaded the moment when kids had to separate from parents and go into Sunday School. The room was loud, the teacher changed often, and one time a boy made fun of Sam for not knowing the memory verse.

No one had ever asked him why it was hard. Once his parents did — with kindness, not correction — Sam admitted his tummy hurt *every* Sunday. Not from church. From worry.

They started previewing what the morning would look like, practiced memory verses together, and even asked if he'd prefer to stay in the main service for a while. No more Sunday cereal catastrophes.

Isla the "Overachiever"

Isla was a teacher's dream. Bright, responsible, high-achieving. But every night at home, she fell apart. Tears, panic over homework, snapping at her siblings. Her parents were baffled — wasn't she thriving?

The truth: Isla's perfectionism was *driven by anxiety*. She worked so hard to avoid making mistakes at school that she was completely emotionally depleted by the time she got home.

They realised she wasn't coping — she was *overcoping*. Together, they created a "decompression window" after school where Isla could relax without pressure. They reassured her that she didn't need to earn love with gold stars. Slowly, she let go of the fear.

Noah's Rude Refusal

When Noah's mum invited a friend over, he scowled and shouted, "I hate people!" and locked himself in his room. The guest was offended. His mum was mortified. But what no one knew was that Noah had experienced bullying in Year 2 — and now any new social situation triggered panic. His rude outburst wasn't defiance — it was defence.

After some digging, his parents began coaching him on what to expect, letting him be in charge of where he played, and giving him time to adjust socially. His confidence grew — and so did his manners.

Each of these stories holds the same truth: Once we understand the *why*, we can change how we respond to the *what*.

What's Really Going On: The Brain, the Body, and the Hidden Work of Anxiety

We've talked a lot about how anxiety *looks* on the outside. Now let's peek under the hood at what's happening inside — not just emotionally, but physiologically. Because anxiety isn't just "in their head." It's in their whole system. At the centre of the anxiety response is a small, almond-shaped structure in the brain called the **a**mygdala. Its job? To detect threat. It's often called the "smoke alarm" of the brain — constantly scanning the environment for danger, and when it perceives one, it fires off signals to the rest of the body.

The problem is, this alarm doesn't know the difference between a real fire and burnt toast. It reacts to anything *that feels dangerous*, whether or not it actually is. Think of Sam on Sunday mornings: His amygdala had paired Sunday School with stress. So even before church began, his brain was sounding the alarm. "Get out! Get safe!" — only it came out as cereal flinging and sock complaints.

Fight, Flight, Freeze (and Fawn)

When the brain perceives danger, it kicks the body into action — what we call the stress response. You may have heard the terms:

- Fight: the child yells, resists, lashes out (like Noah)

- Flight: the child avoids, runs, hides, withdraws

- Freeze: the child goes blank, "zones out," gets stuck

- Fawn: the child becomes overly compliant to avoid conflict or rejection (more common in internalisers like Isla)

Each of these is a nervous system survival strategy. They're not choices — they're reflexes. The child doesn't decide to shout or shut down. Their brain decides for them. When a child is in an anxious state:

- Their heart rate increases

- Muscles tense

- Breathing becomes shallow

- Blood flow shifts away from "thinking" areas of the brain (like the prefrontal cortex) and toward survival functions

This is why anxious kids often struggle to reason or regulate in the moment. The part of their brain that handles logic, planning, and empathy — the "upstairs brain" — goes temporarily offline. When Isla melted down over her homework, it wasn't because she forgot her manners. It was because her brain had been stuck in a low-grade stress response all day. Her nervous system was simply out of capacity.

PSYCH INSIGHT:

Anxiety isn't a behaviour problem — it's a nervous system issue.
A child can't "calm down" on command when their stress system is still activated.

FAITH INSIGHT:

"Be still, and know that I am God." (Psalm 46:10)
Stillness begins with safety. Before we teach truth, we co-create calm.

The Science of Safety: Co-Regulation First

Before a child can self-regulate, they need to co-regulate — to borrow our calm. This means:

- Matching their distress with presence ("I see how upset you are. I'm not going anywhere.")

- Softening your tone and body (calm is contagious)

- Reassuring them that the feeling won't last forever ("Let's ride this wave together.")

We're not excusing the behaviour — we're creating enough safety for the thinking brain to come back online. When Noah lashed out about guests coming over, his parents didn't just discipline — they investigated. They created calm around a trigger. They built a bridge instead of a wall. And his behaviour changed *because* his brain felt safe.

Your calm is the greatest gift you can offer an anxious child. An anxious child doesn't need to be "talked out" of their fear first — they need to feel safe in their body again. That sense of safety isn't something they can create on their own just yet. They learn it first by borrowing it from you. This is what science calls co-regulation: the way a parent or caregiver helps a child return to calm by lending their own calm, steady presence.

Our bodies are wired for emotional resonance — especially in close relationships. This means a child's nervous system often *mirrors* the emotional state of their parent or carer.

- If you're calm, their body begins to settle.

- If you're agitated, their nervous system stays on high alert.

- If you're yelling at them to calm down (we've all been there), their brain hears: *"We're still in danger."*

This isn't your fault. But it *is* your superpower. Co-regulation activates a child's parasympathetic nervous system — the "rest and digest" setting. This slows the heart rate, relaxes muscles, and allows the brain to return to its thinking and reasoning zones. Until this system is activated, a child:

- Can't process logic

- Can't take in correction

- Can't fully hear or trust your words

Co-regulation looks like this:

- Getting close, not bigger
  Sit beside them, not over them. Get on their

level physically.

- Soft voice, soft face, soft breath
Speak slowly. Lower your volume. Relax your shoulders.

- Name what you see without judgment
"I can see your whole body is feeling panicked right now."

- Offer presence over solutions
"I'm here. We'll get through this together."

- Use grounding tools

    - Breathing together: "Let's blow out birthday candles."

    - Touch: hand on shoulder, back rub, or holding hands (if welcomed)

    - Movement: walk, rock, or sway together

Let's go back to Isla. At the end of a school day, her perfectionist anxiety had pushed her brain and body to the limit. She was brittle, not disobedient. Instead of asking "What's wrong with you?" her mum learned to say: "You've had a big day. Let's breathe together. You don't have to explain yet. Let's just sit." In doing that, she helped bring Isla's nervous system back from survival mode. Only *then* did conversation and connection flow.

PSYCH INSIGHT:

Children aren't born knowing how to calm themselves. They learn through repeated, consistent co-regulation with a safe adult. This builds neurological pathways for future self-regulation.

FAITH INSIGHT:

"The Lord is near to the brokenhearted." (Psalm 34:18) God meets us in our emotional storms — not with demands, but with nearness.

5 Steps to Co-Regulation

1 **Get close, not bigger**
Come down to your child's eye level and offer your physical presence.

2 **Soften your voice, face, and breath**
Speak gently, relax your expression, and exhale slowly.

3 **Describe, don't diagnose**
Acknowledge their feelings without questioning or correcting them.

4 **Offer presence over solutions**
Assure them you are there to help them through the distress.

5 **Try grounding techniques**
Use simple tools, like deep breathing or gentle touch.

Jesus didn't just teach calm. He created calm — by meeting people exactly where they were, before they changed, before they understood, before they "got it together." And when someone was anxious, distressed, or stuck in a storm — He never shamed them for it. He came *closer*. If we look at the woman who touched Jesus' robe (Mark 5:25-34), we'll note that she didn't speak. She didn't shout. She didn't ask for healing the "right" way. She reached out — quietly, desperately, from behind. Jesus could have rebuked her for interrupting Him. Instead, He stopped. He turned. He looked.

>"Daughter, your faith has made you well. Go in peace."

He responded to her unspoken distress with honour and affection. He gave her a name — *Daughter.* He gave her peace, not a lecture.

In Mark 9:14-29 we learn of a desperate father who brings his son, who is overwhelmed by seizure like symptoms no one can seem to fix. The crowd is chaotic. The disciples are arguing. The boy falls to the ground, convulsing. Jesus doesn't rush. He asks questions. He listens to the father's fear. And then He gently restores the child. No blame. No frustration. Just steady presence.

"Everything is possible for one who believes," He says.

And the father, beautifully human, replies: *"I do believe. Help me overcome my unbelief!"*

If that's not the cry of every parent watching their child struggle — I don't know what is.

If we examine how Peter walks on water toward Jesus (Matthew 14:22-33) we can assume bravery and a boldness — until he sees the wind and fear floods in. He begins to sink. Jesus doesn't say, "You should've trusted Me." He doesn't say, "You need to get better at this." He reaches out His hand immediately. Yes, He names the fear. Yes, He teaches. But first, He rescues. Over and over again in Scripture, we see the same pattern:

- Compassion first

- Connection before correction

- Calm before teaching

Jesus meets people in storms, caves, tombs, crowded rooms, and lonely hillsides — and always brings them back to peace before asking them to act.

When your child is overwhelmed by a fear they can't name… When their behaviour is frustrating or baffling… When you've repeated yourself a hundred times… Let this be the model:

1. Reach out first
2. Speak softly
3. Look beneath the surface
4. Offer presence before pressure

Let's revisit our three children — now through the lens of Jesus' way.

Sam — The Sunday Meltdown Kid

Sam didn't need a lecture about "respecting socks" or "hurrying up for church."
 He needed someone to ask the right question: *What's happening underneath?* Just like the father who brought his son to Jesus in desperation, Sam's parents slowed down, asked gently, and listened. They didn't correct first — they *connected* first. And in doing so, they helped regulate his nervous system *and* his faith.

Isla — The "Perfect" One Who Crashed at Home

Isla's meltdowns weren't about being spoiled. They were about being spent. Jesus noticed the woman who touched His robe — not because she made a scene, but because He was attuned to quiet distress. Isla needed the same. Her parents learned that silence didn't mean "I'm fine" — it meant, "I don't have words." So they offered rest before rules, grace before grit.

Noah — The Guest-Hating Shouter

Noah's behaviour could have been seen as rude. In fact, it *was* rude — but it was also fearful. His parents followed Jesus' model by looking beyond the outburst to the story behind it. Like Peter sinking in the waves, Noah wasn't trying to make life difficult. He was overwhelmed. And instead of yelling back, they reached out with understanding. Every time you pause to see what's *under* the behaviour — you're doing holy work. You're parenting like Christ. You're choosing mercy over reaction. You're building a house where love is the first language. And over time, this kind of parenting — rooted in truth, neuroscience, and gospel — grows kids who don't just behave better... they *feel safer*.

Reflection & Prayer

Reflect:

- Have I ever corrected my child before I've connected with them?

- Do I sometimes misread their anxiety as bad behaviour?

- What could change in our home if I began seeing beneath the surface?

Prayer:

God,
Thank You for the privilege of seeing into the heart of my child — even when it feels messy, loud, or hard to reach. Help me to slow down and listen more closely. When I'm tired, give me gentleness. When I'm unsure, give me discernment. And when my child is overwhelmed, remind me to be the calm, not the storm. Let my presence reflect Your peace — steady, kind, and safe. Amen.

A Word Over You, Dear Parent

You are not missing it. You are learning to see deeper. You are becoming fluent in a language your child doesn't know how to speak yet. As you learn to recognise anxiety for what it really is — not drama, not rebellion, not weakness — may your heart grow soft and your eyes grow wise. May you no longer feel afraid of the meltdowns, the clinginess, the perfectionism, the rage. May you know that these are not failures to fix — they are signals to guide your love.

God chose *you* to interpret those signals. Not because you're perfect — but because He knew you would show up. Again and again. You are raising a child with big feelings. But you are not doing it alone. God is right here, calming *your* nervous system, too. He sees your efforts. He honours your learning. He's proud of you.

Chapter 4

Teaching Kids to Name and Tame Their Feelings

"I don't like this sandwich!"

That's how it started. A sandwich — a cheese toastie, to be specific — was the flashpoint for a full-blown, tear-streaked, door-slamming storm. Yesterday, it was her favourite. Today, it was "ruined," "disgusting," and apparently the cause of all that was wrong in the world. I'll be honest — I almost lost it too. It was just a sandwich.

But it wasn't really about the sandwich. That's the thing with kids and feelings — what they *say* is wrong often isn't what's *really* going on. The toastie was the tipping point, but underneath it was a build-up of emotion she didn't know how to name. Maybe she'd had a hard day. Maybe someone was unkind at school. Maybe she felt sad and didn't know why. Maybe she was just hungry… for connection. What I'm learning — both as a parent and a clinician — is this: Children can't tame what they can't name. And until they feel safe enough to say what's really going on, they'll keep shouting about sandwiches.

When a child is upset and we offer language for what they're feeling, something powerful happens — not just emotionally, but neurologically. Research shows that naming an emotion reduces its intensity. It activates the part of the brain responsible for language and reasoning (the prefrontal cortex) and helps regulate the amygdala — the part responsible for emotional reactivity. Dr. Dan Siegel calls this "Name it to tame it." It's not about fixing the feeling — it's about making space for it. Giving it a name gives it a boundary. It no longer has to scream to be heard.

But Why Is It So Hard for Kids? Because kids aren't born emotionally literate. They might say "mad" when they mean embarrassed. Or "bored" when they're sad. Or "fine" when they're anything but. Many children have a vocabulary of just three to five emotions — usually happy, sad, mad, and tired. They haven't yet learned to recognise more nuanced emotions like disappointment, jealousy, frustration, guilt, or shame. Worse, many feel unsafe to express "big" feelings — especially if they've been shut down before.

This chapter is about helping you raise a child who doesn't just behave well — but who *understands their own inner world.* A child who can say, "I'm feeling nervous," instead of acting out. A child who can pray, "God, I feel overwhelmed," instead of pretending they're fine. A child who knows: feelings are welcome here.

Zeke was six, and for the last week, every school morning had started with the same refrain: "I don't want to go." Sometimes he said it with a shrug. Sometimes with tears. One morning, he even hid under the bed and refused to come out. His mum tried everything:

- Logical explanations: "School is important."

- Bribery: "There's a treat in your lunchbox!"

- Reassurance: "You'll have fun once you're there."

Nothing changed. On Thursday, after another tearful standoff, she knelt down beside him and asked, *"What does it feel like in your body when you think about school?"* Zeke blinked. He hadn't been asked that before. He mumbled, "My tummy feels twisty." Then she asked, "If that twisty feeling could talk, what would it say?" Zeke paused.

And then, in a whisper: "I'm scared the teacher will ask me to read."

Bingo. That was the moment. It wasn't about school in general. It wasn't about being lazy, dramatic, or stubborn. It was about a very real fear — the kind that lives in the body until someone kind enough helps it find its name. Naming that fear didn't make it vanish. But it made it *manageable*. It turned it from a fog into something they could walk through together.

His mum said, "Thank you for telling me. That makes sense. It's okay to feel nervous about reading out loud. Let's make a plan together." That moment changed everything. Zeke didn't stop being afraid overnight. But now he had a name for what he felt — and a parent who *saw* it. They started using a "feelings check-in" before school, using coloured cards and a feelings chart. Sometimes he chose "worried," sometimes "brave-but-nervous," and sometimes just "tired." But every time he named it, he felt a little more in control.

What once felt like a monster in the dark was now something they could face together — with language, love, and a God who promises to walk us through the scary parts.

"Even though I walk through the darkest valley, I will fear no evil, for You are with me." (Psalm 23:4)

Parent Prompt:
Can you remember a time your child resisted something — and you later realised there was a deeper feeling underneath? What might they be trying to say with their behaviour, that they don't yet have words for?

What could happen if, next time, you paused and simply asked: *"What does it feel like in your body right now?"*

It had been a hard morning. The kind where everything felt one size too heavy — news I didn't expect, a few too many responsibilities, and a general sense of being stretched too thin. I was standing in the kitchen, staring blankly at the dishes, trying to pretend I was fine. Because that's what we do sometimes, isn't it? We tuck it in, smooth it over, tell ourselves, *Just keep going.*

Then my son burst into the room, glowing with pride, carrying a Lego creation. "Mum, look what I made!" he beamed. I smiled — or at least I thought I did. But he stopped in his tracks, frowned slightly, and asked, "Why do you look a little bit sad?" I wanted to brush it off. Say something cheerful. Praise the Lego and move on. But his question landed softly and squarely on my heart.

So I crouched down beside him and said, "I've had a bit of a hard day. I think I'm just feeling a little tired and sad. But seeing what you built — that really brightened things up." He nodded thoughtfully, then placed the Lego carefully in front of me. "You can keep this one if you want. It's a cheering-up robot."

I realised that emotional honesty — even just a little — doesn't weigh down our kids. It teaches them empathy. It shows them that feelings are allowed. That sadness isn't dangerous. And that love still fits inside hard days.

Fear rarely introduces itself politely. Children don't usually say, "Mum, I'm experiencing an internal threat response due to unresolved social anxiety." They slam the door. They scream about socks. They dig in their heels and shout, "I hate this!" And because fear doesn't always *look* like fear, it's often misunderstood — by teachers, by siblings, by parents who love their kids deeply but are running low on sleep and patience. Instead of saying "I'm afraid," a child might say: "This is stupid." "I don't want to." "Everyone's looking at me."

Or… nothing at all. Just a meltdown in the carpark.

Below are some everyday stories — fictionalised based on cases I've encountered, that show how fear *hides in plain sight*. You may see your child in one of them. Or maybe, like me, you'll see a moment you once missed… and feel the gentle nudge of grace.

Luca was 9 and had always been slow to warm up in social situations. So when his mum told him they were going to a birthday party, he crossed his arms and growled, "I'm not going. It's boring and I hate parties." The truth? He didn't hate parties. He feared walking into a crowded room, not knowing who to talk to, and feeling like the odd one out. But he didn't have words for that.

So instead of saying *"I'm afraid I won't fit in,"* he screamed, slammed the bedroom door, and refused to come out. His little sister was already dressed and excited — now she was crying because the party might be cancelled. His mum felt torn between kids. Guilt. Frustration. Embarrassment. What looked like *attitude* was actually social anxiety.

Jada was usually a rule-follower. But every time her class did group presentations, she'd start acting out in the lead-up. She got in trouble for interrupting the teacher, refusing to participate, and making silly faces at classmates.

Her teacher said, "She's being disruptive." But at home, Jada broke down and sobbed, "I don't want to talk in front of everyone. What if I forget my words?" Her parents had assumed she was being cheeky. In reality, her behaviour was a panic response — an attempt to avoid a terrifying moment.

Noah's family went to the park nearly every Saturday. But last month, a dog had run up to him unexpectedly. It didn't hurt him — just barked and sniffed — but since then, every park trip had ended in screaming, refusal to get out of the car, and yelling at his parents: "You never listen! I said I don't want to go!" The dog wasn't there anymore. But his fear was. And it was dictating his tone, his body, and the whole family's schedule.

Ella was terrified of being sick. After a tummy bug last year, she became hyperaware of hygiene. Now, if her younger brother sneezed near her, she screamed. If she touched a doorknob, she ran to the bathroom. And if someone mentioned vomit — even casually — she'd panic. Her parents tried reasoning. Explaining germs. They'd say, "You're fine. It's not a big deal." But in her body, it *was* a big deal. She wasn't trying to control the family. She was trying to feel safe. Eventually, dinner routines, school drop-offs, and even visiting relatives became a battleground. Her fear ruled the room.

Every morning before school, Theo clung to his mum like Velcro. When the bell rang, he screamed, kicked, or froze. Teachers started describing him as "too attached." He began complaining of stomachaches. But what no one saw was this: Theo didn't know how to manage the flood of emotion that came with separating from his safe person. His fear didn't look like tears — it looked like chaos. At home, the stress spread. His mum felt guilty and exhausted. His dad, who didn't understand the depth of it, said, "You just need to be firmer." The whole household became tense around mornings.

Key Takeaway Across All These Stories:

- Fear is sneaky. It wears costumes: defiance, control, tantrums, avoidance.

- Fear doesn't sound like *"I'm afraid."* It sounds like *"This is stupid!"* or *"You're mean!"* or *"I hate this!"*

- These behaviours impact everyone: siblings, parents, teachers.

- Families often feel isolated, frustrated, or judged — especially when others don't see the fear behind the fire.

Jesus and Emotional Honesty

If the Son of God could weep, your child is allowed to cry. Sometimes Christian parents are hesitant to make too much space for emotion. We worry we'll encourage self-pity or weakness, or that we should just teach our children to "trust God and be joyful." But here's the truth: Jesus didn't suppress emotion — He expressed it. Freely, fully, and without shame.

Jesus Wept (John 11:35)

Shortest verse in the Bible. One of the most profound.

At the tomb of Lazarus, even knowing resurrection was moments away, Jesus stood in the pain of the people He loved — and wept. He didn't rush to the solution. He didn't say, "No need to cry, I'm about to fix this." He stopped and entered into the grief. His tears were not a lack of faith. They were an expression of *love*.

Matthew 26:36–39 tells us the night before His crucifixion, Jesus — knowing what was ahead — didn't power through in silence. He cried out to His Father.

"My soul is overwhelmed with sorrow to the point of death."

"If it is possible, let this cup pass from Me."

Those are not the words of a spiritually weak person. Those are the words of someone showing courageous honesty with God. Even as He submitted to the Father's will, Jesus didn't pretend He was okay. He brought His full emotional experience to God — and trusted that it was safe to do so. Jesus Made Space for Others' Emotions:

- He didn't tell the woman who wept at His feet to pull herself together.

- He didn't hush the man who cried out, "Have mercy on me!"

- He didn't rush the bleeding woman who had suffered in silence for twelve years.

- He noticed. He listened. He made space.

He never said, "That's not a big deal." He said, "Your faith has healed you," and *"I see you."*

I think for us, it means our kids need the freedom to be emotional and faithful. They can cry, struggle, question, and still love God. They can feel deeply and still belong. They can say, *"I'm scared"*, and still be growing in courage. If Jesus could express sorrow, your child can too. And if Jesus could sit with pain before offering peace, so can we.

🧠 PSYCH INSIGHT:

Children are wired to co-regulate and to mirror the emotional openness of the adults around them. When you model healthy emotional expression — naming your own feelings, staying regulated through theirs — it builds neural pathways that support lifelong emotional intelligence.

📖 FAITH INSIGHT:

Jesus didn't reject emotional expression — He embodied it. He grieved, groaned, wept, and rejoiced openly. Our children reflect the image of a God who feels. Teaching them emotional honesty isn't weakness — it's spiritual formation.

The Feelings Wheel - a map for the heart.

When kids get overwhelmed, their language often shrinks to just a few default words:

> "I'm mad."
> "I'm fine."
> "I don't know."

But beneath those words is a whole spectrum of emotion they haven't learned how to name yet. That's where the Feelings Wheel comes in — a simple tool that expands a child's emotional vocabulary and helps them identify *what they're really feeling*.

From a psychological and neurological standpoint, naming a feeling:

- Activates the prefrontal cortex (the "thinking brain")

- Lowers amygdala activity (the "alarm bell" of anxiety)

- Creates cognitive distance from the emotion so it feels less overwhelming

"Name it to tame it" isn't just a cute phrase — it's a brain-calming practice.

How to Use It with Kids

1. Print a child-friendly feelings wheel (like the one below or you can draw your own, buy one, or grab a free printable online)
2. Keep it visible — on the fridge, beside the breakfast table, in a calm-down corner.
3. Do regular "check-ins":

    o "Which word fits how your day felt?"

    o "Which colour do you feel in your body right now?"

    o "Point to one for me — I'll help you read it."

4. Validate, don't fix:

    o "You're feeling disappointed? That makes sense."

- "It's okay to feel nervous about something new."

- "I feel that way too sometimes."

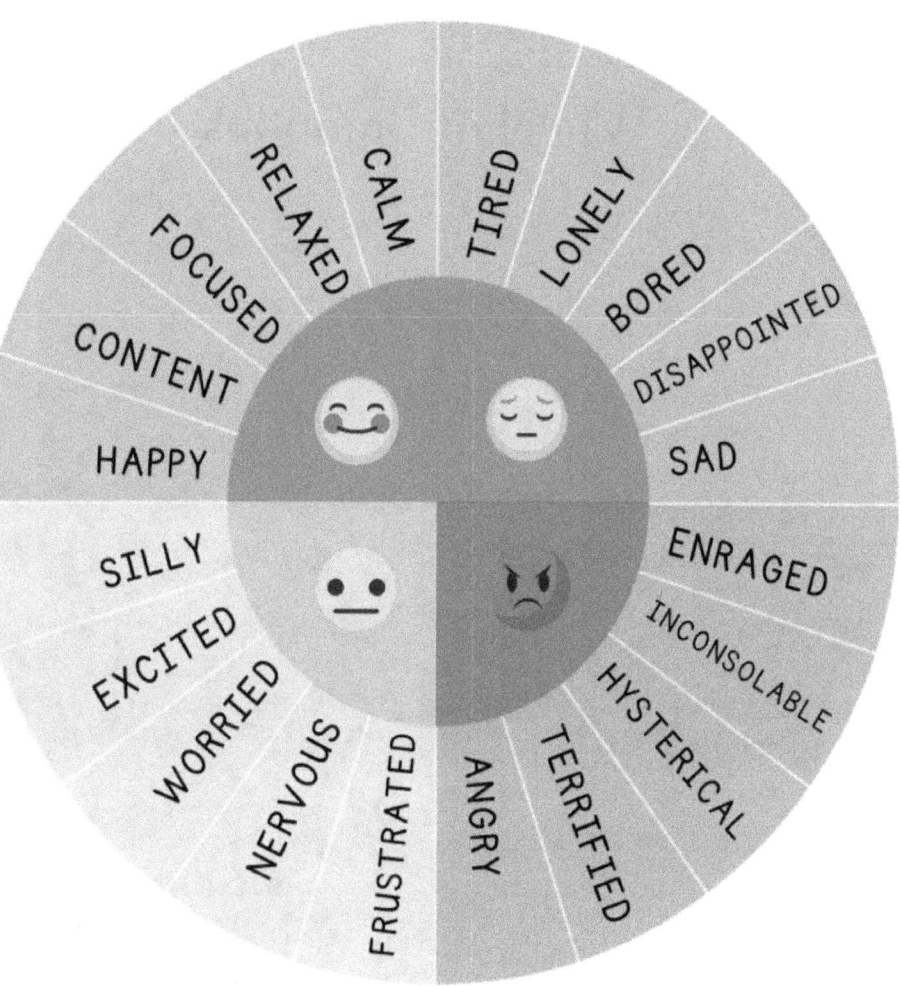

- Wheel of Emotions -

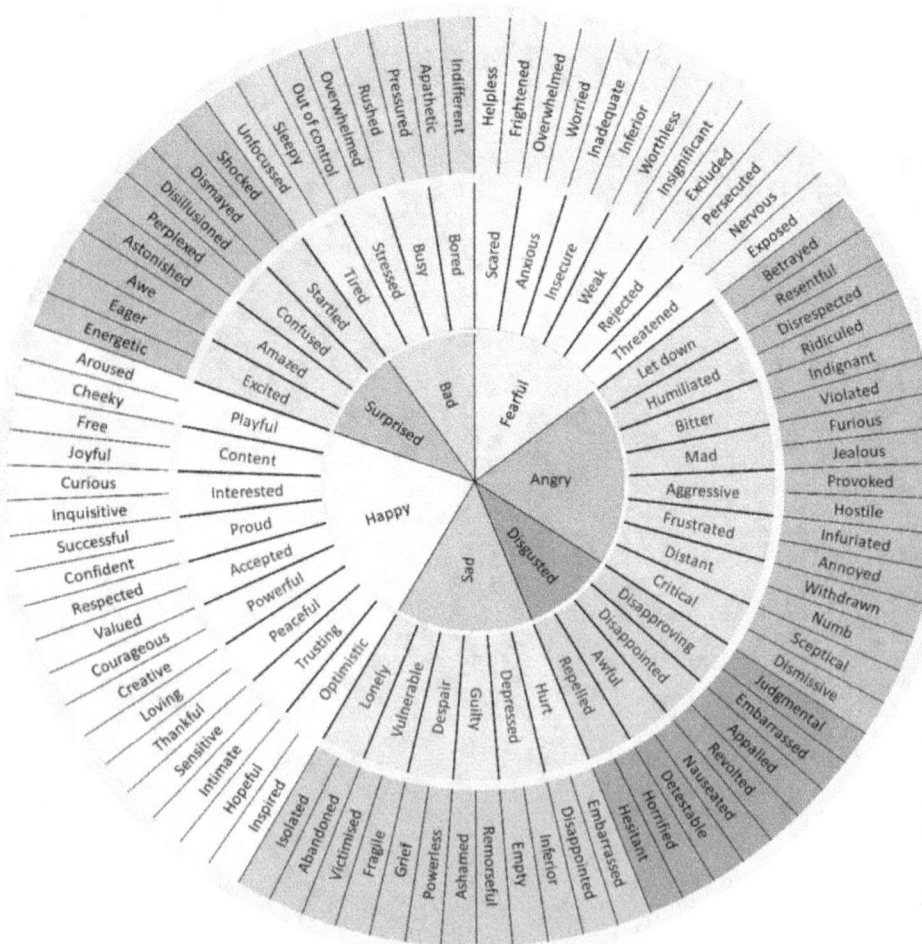

Have the child select a base emotion (they are more likely able to identify with these) and then ask them to see if there's a feeling that extends out from that within the colour category that might also apply - this will help them build deeper emotional literacy. If there is no word listed that applies to them, see if they can come up with one to add.

Pre- Bedtime Feelings Check-In

This is one of my favourite simple practices. Each afternoon, way before the bedtime routine, ask your child:

- What's one feeling you had today?

- When did you feel it?

- What did you need in that moment?

You can even go first to model it: "Today I felt... frustrated, when the printer jammed again. I needed a deep breath and a moment to reset." This creates emotional fluency through repetition and safety. You're not just talking about feelings — you're *discipling the heart*. The reason I suggest to do it before the nightly bedtime routine, is sometimes this conversation can prompt a larger conversation that you might feel like rushing through to get on with bedtime.

When our kids are overwhelmed, we often want to help quickly — to fix, reassure, or redirect the behaviour. But in doing so, we sometimes bypass the *feeling underneath*. Below are common phrases parents say when children express big emotions — and a reframed response that makes space for those feelings while still holding healthy boundaries.

1. **"You're fine."**
Translation to a child: I'm not allowed to feel this.

Try instead:

> "That looked scary. I'm here."
> "You're safe now. Want to tell me what hurt?"
> "Even if it's small, your feelings matter to me."

2. **"There's nothing to be afraid of."**
Translation to a child: You're overreacting. Stop it.

Try instead:

"I get why that felt scary to you. Want to sit with me a minute?"

"It's okay to feel nervous — we'll figure it out together."

"You don't have to be brave alone."

3. "Calm down!"
Translation to a child: Your emotions are a problem.

Try instead:

"I'm right here. Let's breathe together."

"This is big. I see it. You're not in trouble — we'll ride this wave together."

"Let's find some calm together first, then we can talk."

4. "Stop being so dramatic."
Translation to a child: You're too much.

Try instead:

"Looks like this is feeling *really* big for you."

"Want to help me name what's going on inside?"

"Let's figure out what your feelings are trying to tell us."

5. "Don't be silly." *(often said about fears)*
Translation to a child: What you feel is stupid.

Try instead:

"It's okay to feel worried. Everyone gets scared sometimes."
"That moth surprised you, didn't it? Let's talk about it when your body feels safer."
"Even if I'm not scared of it, I believe that you are — and I want to help."

6. "Go to your room until you can calm down."
Translation to a child: You're only allowed around me when you're regulated.

Try instead:

"I'm here with you while this feeling moves through."
"We can take a break together. Let's find your calm corner or your comfort tool."

"Would it help to sit close or do something with our hands?"

This isn't about making parents feel guilty, and don't worry, I've said all these too when pressed for time or too tired to pause. It's about helping us see how *our words shape our children's inner world* — and how small shifts can make a big impact.

But what about when a child or young teen has a monumental reaction to what is literally a small problem... isn't it reasonable that I help them see it isn't a big deal? Well...Yes — there is absolutely room for *both* reframing and co-regulating, but the key is timing and tone. When a 10- or 12-year-old completely loses it over a broken pencil, the "wrong" socks, or their sibling breathing near them, it can feel baffling. You may wonder, *"Surely they know this isn't a big deal?"* But in that moment, their thinking brain is offline — and their emotional brain is in charge.

So here's the golden rule: Co-regulate first. Reframe later.

Step 1: Co-Regulate First

You don't need to agree with the size of the reaction — but you need to join the nervous system, not argue with it.

Say things like:

- "That really threw you, huh?"

- "Let's just breathe and sit together for a sec."

- "I can tell this is a 10 out of 10 for you right now."

This says: *I see you. You're not bad. I'm not afraid of your big feelings.* Even if the issue seems small, your child is showing you that it feels *big in their body*. They need to come back to safety before anything else.

Step 2: Reframe Gently (After the Storm)

Once calm is restored, *then* we reframe. In therapeutic terms, *reframing* is the process of gently helping someone see a thought, feeling, or situation from a different — often more helpful — perspective. It doesn't mean pretending a problem isn't real. It means adding context, insight, or compassion so that the emotion doesn't stay stuck in its original form. For children, reframing might sound like: *"It wasn't that you were rude — it was that you were scared, and didn't have the words."* Or, *"Maybe it's not that your friend hates you — maybe she had a hard day too."* Reframing helps the child move from shame or helplessness toward self-awareness, empathy, and problem-solving. Over time, it becomes a tool they learn to use on their own, which is a major goal of emotional maturity. Some examples of what you might say to help prompt reframing for you child could be:

- "Let's talk about what made that moment feel so big."

- "Do you think the broken pencil was the whole story, or was something else already building up?"

- "How could we catch those big feelings earlier next time, before they spill out?"

This helps older children develop metacognition — thinking about their thinking — and begin to *link triggers, stress, and reactions.* We're not ignoring the behaviour. We're building the bridge between their emotion and their awareness.

🧠 PSYCH INSIGHT:
Reframing activates the prefrontal cortex — the part of the brain responsible for logic, reflection, and regulation. When we reframe a thought or feeling, we're literally rewiring the brain's emotional pathways toward greater flexibility and resilience.

📖 FAITH INSIGHT:
Romans 12:2 encourages us to "be transformed by the renewing of your mind." Reframing is one way we help our children practice this — learning to see themselves, others, and their struggles through the lens of grace, not guilt.

Even Jesus had moments when small things carried big weight. A fig tree not bearing fruit. A temple out of order. His emotions were never "too much" — they were rooted in meaning. We can help our kids understand their *why* — with patience, not punishment.

Parent Reflection:

- When my child has a "big reaction," what's my first instinct — to correct, to calm, or to connect?

- Do I tend to interpret emotional outbursts as disrespect — or could they be distress in disguise?

- How might I offer a new way of seeing, instead of just stopping the behaviour?

Ask God:
Lord, help me see past the noise of the moment. Teach me to speak truth with tenderness — not to shame, but to guide. And when I forget, give me grace to try again.

Everyday Habits for Emotional Fluency

Emotional understanding doesn't happen in one conversation. It grows in the soil of everyday moments — car rides, bedtime chats, post-meltdown cuddles, and dinner-table stories.

Here are simple ways to nurture emotional fluency in your home:

1. Model Naming Your Own Feelings

"I feel a little frustrated right now. I'm going to take a few breaths."
 "I felt really thankful today when you helped your sister."

You're teaching: *feelings are normal, nameable, and manageable.*

2. Use Emotion Cards or a Check-In Chart
 Make it visual. Let kids point to how they feel — even just with colours. (Green = calm, yellow = silly, red = angry, blue = sad.)

3. Tell "Feeling Stories" at Bedtime
 Instead of "What did you do today?", try:

> "What was one big feeling you had today?"
> "Was there a moment you felt proud? Embarrassed? Worried?"

4. Use Books, Shows, and Bible Stories as Teaching Tools

> "How do you think David felt when he faced Goliath?"
> "What would you have done if you were Joseph in the well?"

"How do you think that character felt when they were left out?"

5. Celebrate Emotional Bravery

"That was really brave, telling me you were nervous."
"I'm proud of you for naming how you felt — even when it was hard."

When we praise emotional honesty, we make it a strength, not a shame.

Closing Prayer

God,
Thank You for the feelings You placed in our children — not by accident, but by design.
Help me to see their anger, fear, and sadness not as threats to manage, but as windows into their hearts. Teach me to slow down, speak softly, and listen well.
Let my words be like water to thirsty soil. Grow in me the patience to name, reframe, and remain present — even on the messy days. And when I miss it, thank You for always giving me another try. Amen.

A Word Over You, Dear Parent

You are doing sacred work. Every time you pause, every time you say, "Tell me more," every time you kneel to eye-level instead of raise your voice — you're planting seeds. You're raising a child who doesn't have to hide their emotions. A child who can look at their own heart with gentleness. A child who believes God is safe — because *you* were safe. You don't have to get it right every time. You just have to keep showing up, willing to learn. Your own emotional growth is part of their healing. And through it all, the God who feels deeply, who weeps and rejoices and sees every tear, is parenting with you.

You've got this. And even when you don't — He's still got you.

Chapter 5

Why Avoidance Feels Good (But Makes Anxiety Worse)

Helping kids face fears with courage and grace

There was a season when my daughter wouldn't walk past the house with the dog.

To be fair, the dog had got out and ran at us — once — weeks earlier. It didn't bite, growl, or even get close. But it *startled* her, and her nervous system recorded the event in permanent marker. So the next time we walked that way and saw the dog in the front yard, she froze. Tears welled up. Her little fists clenched. "Mum, I can't. Let's go the long way." We were already running late. The long way added ten minutes. But her panic was so real, so physical, that I caved and said, "Okay, not today." Instantly, her whole body relaxed. She chatted the rest of the walk. He even smiled. And my brain whispered: *Phew. That was easier.*

The next day? Same request. "Let's take the long way." The day after that? She started scanning for dogs on every street. Soon, she didn't want to walk at all. That's when I realised: We hadn't just avoided the dog. We'd trained her brain to expect fear — and to trust avoidance.

Why Avoidance Works (for a While)

Avoidance offers instant relief. It's the nervous system's way of saying, "We're uncomfortable. Let's not do that again." And when we avoid the thing that caused stress, the brain says, "Thank you. You kept me safe." It rewards us with a quick burst of calm. The problem is, the brain never gets a chance to update the story. It doesn't learn, "*That dog was actually behind a fence.*" It doesn't learn, *"I can give a talk and survive."* It only learns, *"That was scary. And we escaped."* And so anxiety stays alive. Sometimes it even grows. Avoidance is the glue that holds anxiety in place.

Parent Reflection:

- Can I think of a time when I helped my child avoid something that scared them — just to keep the peace, or because I felt unsure what else to do?

- What message might my child have received from that moment?

- Have I ever found myself relieved when something anxiety-triggering got cancelled — and then felt conflicted about it?

We're not judging those moments. We're just noticing them — with compassion and curiosity. Avoidance feels like kindness in the moment. And sometimes, it *is* a wise choice. But as we grow in understanding, we learn that helping our children move *through* fear — not just around it — is a deeper kind of love.

Ask God:
Father, help me discern when to comfort, when to challenge, and when to walk beside. Show me how to gently lead my child toward courage, without shame — and without fear leading the way.

Anxiety isn't just a feeling — it's a loop. And once that loop is in motion, it can quietly shape a child's world.

Let's walk through it again, this time from the lens of avoidance:

1. A Trigger Appears
   The child faces something that feels threatening — a barking dog, a spelling test, a busy birthday party.

2. Anxiety Shows Up
   Their brain's alarm system fires up. Heart races, tummy hurts, thoughts swirl:
   "I can't do this. What if something bad happens?"

3. Avoidance Feels Like Safety
   They escape the situation. Relief floods in. Everyone calms down.

4. Relief Reinforces the Avoidance
   The brain says, *"Good job. You stayed safe by running away."*
   The child learns: *Avoidance = Safety.*

5. Fear Grows Over Time
   The next time the situation arises, it feels *even scarier*. The avoidance loop tightens.

Every time anxiety is avoided, the fear grows a little bigger — and the child's world gets a little smaller.

From Avoidance to Approach: A Biblical Model of Courage

The world often defines courage as being fearless — leaping headfirst into danger with grit and glory. But biblical courage looks different. It doesn't ignore fear. It names it, faces it, and then takes the next small step — *with God.*

> "Be strong and courageous. Do not be afraid or terrified… for the Lord your God goes with you."
> — *Deuteronomy 31:6*

In the Bible, the most courageous people weren't the ones with the biggest muscles or the loudest voices. They were the ones who chose to walk forward even while trembling. Peter didn't walk on water because he felt confident. He stepped out because Jesus called him — and he trusted that Jesus was bigger than the waves. Was he anxious? Very likely. Did he doubt? Yes — and he sank a little. But Jesus didn't shame him. He caught him. And sometimes, that's what

bravery looks like: A half-step forward, a wobble...
and the reassurance of God's grip.

David didn't start by fighting giants. He started by protecting sheep. Facing lions. Practising trust in small, hidden places. God trained his courage *before* the battlefield. And when the moment came, David brought not just a sling, but a testimony:

> "The Lord who delivered me from the lion and the bear will deliver me from this Philistine."
> — *1 Samuel 17:37*

Courage isn't the absence of fear. It's the choice to move forward, in tiny faithful steps, *with fear present.* Helping our children build courage means supporting them to take *just the next step* (not the whole journey at once) and reminding them of *Who goes with them. Its about* believing that God can use even a shaky voice or sweaty palms for His glory. Courage is built in the doing — not the avoiding. And we get to be the calm voice that says "It's okay to be scared. Let's do this together. God's got you."

> **🧠 PSYCH INSIGHT:**
> When a child repeatedly avoids something that triggers anxiety, the brain strengthens the fear circuit. But when they face that fear in small, manageable doses — and discover they can survive it — the brain begins to rewire. This process is called exposure in clinical psychology. With each successful step, the brain updates its story from "danger" to "safe enough."
>
> **📖 FAITH INSIGHT:**
> Scripture never denies fear — it speaks into it. God consistently meets people in the moment of action, not before. Moses found his voice while speaking. Esther found her courage as she approached the king. Courage grows when we move forward in faith, not when we wait to feel fearless.

What is the antidote to avoidance? In therapy, exposure is a structured process that helps someone gradually face what they fear — starting small, moving step by step, and building confidence with each repetition. It's the opposite of avoidance. And it's one of the most effective ways to reduce anxiety long term.

But exposure isn't about throwing kids into the deep end or pushing past their limits. It's about creating opportunities to face fear with support, in a way that teaches their brain: *"I can do this. I am safe. I am stronger than I thought — and I'm not alone."* We're not trying to eliminate fear overnight. We're trying to build tolerance — one small success at a time.

Helping your child face their fears doesn't mean pushing them past the edge of panic.
It means walking slowly and safely toward the fear — together. We call this gentle exposure — a series of small, supported steps that build confidence and shrink anxiety.

Think of it like teaching your child to swim: You don't toss them into the deep end. You help them dip a toe in, then stand waist-deep, then float, then paddle — with you close by the whole time.

Step-by-Step: Exposure in Action

Let's walk through an example. Situation: Your child fears public speaking.

Step 1: Start small, away from the trigger. Talk about what they're afraid might happen: *"What feels scary about talking in front of others?"*

Step 2: Break the fear into tiny pieces. E.g., writing down a sentence, saying it aloud at home, recording themselves on video, reading to a family member, presenting to a pet.

Step 3: Practise — repeatedly, calmly, and positively. Let them feel a small amount of discomfort and come out the other side.

Step 4: Celebrate small wins; "You didn't want to even try last week, and now you read to Dad! That's courage growing."

Step 5: Move to real-life situations. Sign up for a low-pressure group project. Practice at school assembly. Invite feedback from a trusted teacher.

Here are some other examples of gentle Exposure dependent on the specific fear;

Fear of dogs
Step-by-step:

1. Look at dog pictures

2. Watch a dog behind a fence

3. Stand across the street from a dog

4. Visit a calm dog with an adult present

5. Pet a dog on the back (when ready)

Fear of social events
Step-by-step:

1. Talk about what to expect

2. Drive by the venue

3. Stay for 5 minutes

4. Bring a comfort item

5. Set a "brave goal" — say hi to one person

LADDER OF EXPOSURE
Practicing Brave for New Challenges

When to Pause, When to Push

How to tell if your child is ready to take the next brave step? Supporting a child through anxiety is a delicate dance between compassion and courage. Go too fast, and they shut down. Go too slow, and anxiety settles in like an unwanted guest. So how do we know when to pause... and when to gently nudge forward?

When to Pause

It's wise to pause if:

- Your child is dysregulated (crying, panicking, or frozen)

- They can't hear or process your words in the moment

- They refuse with fear, not just preference ("I won't" vs. "I can't")

- You're feeling overwhelmed and can't co-regulate calmly

- You sense pushing would break trust, not build confidence

Pausing isn't failing. It's protecting the connection — which is the foundation for all future bravery. When you pause, try this: "This feels too big right now. Let's step back and try again another day." "You're not in trouble. We'll figure it out together."

When to Push (Gently)

Consider encouraging the next step when:

- Your child is mildly uncomfortable but still engaged

- They show curiosity, even if they're hesitant

- They've already succeeded at a smaller step and need help stretching

- You're calm, prepared, and have time to support them well

Gentle pushing looks like: "This next step might feel wobbly — but I'll be with you the whole time." "You've done hard things before, and I've seen how strong you are."
"Let's try for 2 minutes, then you can decide if we keep going."

The Golden Rule: *Connection First, Progress Second*

Progress in anxiety recovery doesn't come from pushing harder. It comes from your child learning to trust you in the fear — and beginning to trust themselves. You'll know you're in the right zone when they're a little nervous, but still moving, you're both still breathing, and they recover faster each time, even if they wobble. Avoidance shrinks the world. But connection gives them a *bridge* to something bigger.

What Helps Most?

- Stay calm and regulated yourself — even if they panic

- Let them lead the pace (but don't avoid completely)

- Use language that frames fear as something they can handle

Say: "This will feel tricky — but you're safe, and I'm here." "Bravery doesn't mean you don't feel scared. It means you showed up anyway." "Let's do this together, one step at a time."

WHEN TO PAUSE, WHEN TO PUSH

IS MY CHILD READY TO TAKE THE NEXT STEP?

PAUSE?

- Feelings are too big to process
- Shutting down or panicking
- Refusing with fear ("I can't")
- Needs help to regulate
- Pushing might hurt trust

PUSH?

- A little neryous, but curious
- Showing signs of progress
- Resisted, but still engaged
- Calm enough to try
- Ready for a small stretch

PRIORITIZE CONNECTION — WITHOUT HURRYING

CHAPTER 6

WHEN WORRY BECOMES THE BOSS: HELPING KIDS MANAGE CONTROL AND PERFECTIONISM

Cultivating peace when anxiety masquerades as 'good behaviour'

One of the children I once worked with — let's call her Grace — was eight years old and the kind of student every teacher dreams of. Polite. Focused. Exceptionally neat handwriting. But her mum brought her to see me because afternoons were becoming impossible. One day, Grace had a school project due: a "design your own rocket ship" craft. She had chosen silver glitter, star stickers, and an array of perfectly sorted pom poms. Everything was going well — until one pom pom went on crooked. Grace peeled it off. Re-glued it. Peeled it again. Eventually, she burst into tears, sobbing, *"I can't get it right! It's ruined!"*

Her mum tried to help. Grace refused. Later, when we spoke about it, Grace said quietly, *"If I hand it in looking messy, maybe my teacher will think I'm not smart anymore."* This wasn't a tantrum. It was a fear response — polished, perfection-shaped, and exhausting. Some kids express anxiety by avoiding. Others by acting out. But some — like Grace — respond by *trying harder*.

They:

- Follow the rules to the letter

- Ask for reassurance constantly

- Crumble when plans change

- Panic over anything less than perfect

At first, they seem like "the easy ones." But beneath their well-behaved exterior is a nervous system working overtime to keep control. Perfectionism Is a Costume Worry Wears. Perfectionism isn't about pride. It's about fear. It says, *"If I'm flawless, I'll be safe. I'll be enough. I won't disappoint anyone."* Children with anxious perfectionism:

- Struggle to rest unless everything is "just right"

- Blame themselves harshly for small mistakes

- Fear failure not because of laziness — but because of love and longing

They want to do well. But more than that, they want to feel *secure*. In this chapter, we'll talk about:

- Why some kids use control and perfectionism to manage anxiety

- How to help them loosen their grip gently

- What Jesus taught us about effort, rest, and grace

- How to parent in a way that praises *courage*, not just *compliance*

Because God never called our children — or us — to be perfect. He called us to trust Him, even when the glue stick is crooked.

The Quiet Face of Anxiety: When Worry Looks Like Obedience.

Some children yell when they're anxious. Others withdraw. But there's a quieter group — the ones who try to hold it all together. They do their homework. They remember their hat for school (ugh, what's that like?). They keep the peace at the dinner table.

And sometimes, they seem like they don't *need* much. But if you look closely, you'll see it... the tears over a misplaced homework sheet, the panic when plans change unexpectedly, the tension in their shoulders when they make a mistake. Or the endless need for reassurance: *"Is this okay? Did I do it right?"* They're not trying to be dramatic. They're trying to stay safe.

In psychological terms, this is called internalising anxiety — when fear is turned inward, rather than acted out. These children often:

- Mask their emotions in public

- Appear mature beyond their years

- Experience physical symptoms (tummy aches, fatigue, nail biting)

- Avoid risk in case they fail

And because their distress doesn't *disrupt* the world around them, it can easily go unnoticed — until it builds up silently. I once worked with a mum who said of her daughter, *"She's just a perfectionist. She likes things neat."* But the more we unpacked her daughter's behaviour, the more it became clear: This wasn't a preference. It was a *compulsion*. She wasn't tidying for fun. She was tidying for relief. For control. For calm. She wasn't striving for excellence. She was afraid of disappointing someone — afraid of letting herself down.

That's when we both realised: What looked like maturity was actually a signal. Not "she's thriving." But *"she's managing — and it's taking everything she has."*

Parent Reflection:

- Does my child ever seem "too" well-behaved — like they're holding their breath through life?

- Have I noticed signs of anxiety masked as helpfulness, order, or rule-following?

- Do I praise my child more for their achievements than for their honesty or effort?

Take a moment to ask:

What might my child be carrying quietly, that I haven't noticed?
Is there space in our home for mistakes, mess, and "off" days — without fear of disappointing me?

And if the answer feels heavy, remember: It's never too late to change the tone of your home — to shift from performance to presence.

Ask God:

Lord, help me see past the tidy surface.
Let me be a safe place where my child doesn't have to hold it all together.
Teach me to delight in who they are — not what they do.

And teach me the same about myself, too.
Amen.

Why Some Kids Try to Stay in Control (And What It Costs Them)

When the world feels uncertain, some children reach for the only thing they can manage: control. They control their routines. They control their schoolwork. They control their food, their clothes, their creative projects, the way their books are stacked on the shelf.

And often, they try to control *how others see them* — polite, kind, competent, no trouble. It's not manipulation. It's self-protection. For an anxious child, control becomes the brain's favourite tool. When something feels unpredictable — a test, a loud environment, a surprise visit — their nervous system starts scanning for threat. And when they feel out of control on the inside, they try to fix it on the outside. So they re-do their homework three times, ask "What time are we leaving?" fourteen times, line their toys up in colour order, double-check everything: *"Are you mad at me? Did I do it right?"*

It *soothes* them — temporarily. But here's the cost:

They begin to believe that the world is only safe if they're in control. And that's a heavy burden for a child to carry.

What It Costs Them

When worry becomes the boss, children lose access to Playfulness — everything feels serious, Flexibility — surprises feel threatening, Self-kindness — every mistake feels like failure, and, Spiritual peace — they begin to believe love is earned, not given. Eventually, anxiety begins to shape their identity: "I'm the good one." "I'm the one who never messes up." "I'm only valuable when I get it right." And that's not what God intended.

Perfectionism feels like control. But really, it's a disguise that fear wears. A child who needs everything "just right" isn't being fussy. They're often trying to avoid something that feels even worse than imperfection - disappointment. Or disapproval, shame, being misunderstood, failing at something that *matters*. In their mind, if they can get it perfect, they'll stay ahead of the pain. The Problem? Perfection doesn't keep us safe... It only keeps us busy. Children who cling to perfection may avoid tasks and activities where they feel there's a risk of failure, such as starting a drawing in case it "looks silly", handing in homework unless it's flawless, speaking up in class because they might get it wrong, or participating in messy or creative activities — too unpredictable.

And because perfection isn't possible, these kids are left feeling tired, self-critical, overwhelmed, alone. And perhaps worst of all... afraid that if they can't do it perfectly, they'll disappoint someone they love. What they need instead? They need to hear: "Your worth isn't in your work." "You're not loved for what you get right." "God's peace doesn't depend on your performance — and neither does mine." Because perfection isn't peace. And safety doesn't come from flawless behaviour. It comes from grace — the kind that says, *You're okay, even when you get it wrong.*

When a child's brain experiences frequent anxiety, the amygdala (the brain's smoke alarm) becomes hypersensitive to any sign of unpredictability or failure. To calm this internal threat system, the child may develop rigid thinking, perfectionism, or controlling behaviours — all in an attempt to prevent discomfort. While these strategies offer short-term relief, they reinforce the brain's belief that safety = performance. Over time, this can limit flexibility, curiosity, and joy. Jesus never demanded perfection. He met people in their limitations — the woman caught in sin, the disciples who doubted, the children who fidgeted. In Matthew 11:28, He says:

> "Come to me, all who are weary and burdened, and I will give you rest."

Perfectionism is a burden. Jesus offers *rest* — even (and especially) when we haven't got it all together.

Tyson was ten, and fast. Fast enough to make the local rep footy team. Fast enough that his coach called him "our golden boy." But week after week, Tyson would leave practice furious, throw his gear across the room, and say things like, "I messed everything up. I'm hopeless." "If I can't get picked for first position, I'm a nobody."

His parents brought him to counselling thinking he had "anger issues." But underneath the slammed doors and harsh self-talk was a child terrified of not being enough. We traced it back: A coach who praised performance, not perseverance, a dad (well-meaning and loving) who celebrated wins more than effort, a perfectionistic brain that turned every mistake into a full-body threat response.

Tyson didn't need a stricter routine. He needed permission to be a kid again — to try, to fail, and to still be fully loved. One day, when he sat fidgeting with his shin guards, I said, "What would happen if you had a bad game?" He looked up and whispered, "Then who would I be?" And that's when I knew: This wasn't about sport. It was about identity. His sense of worth was tied to performance, not presence.

Parent Prompt

- Have I ever seen my child unravel after a small failure — even when I didn't expect them to?

- Does my child define themselves by what they *do* — their sport, their grades, their helpfulness — rather than who they *are*?

- How do I respond when they make mistakes? Do I lead with empathy, or urgency?

Take a quiet moment and ask:

Lord, show me if I've accidentally praised performance over peace.
Teach me to speak identity over my child — not because they've earned it, but because You've already given it.

Let my home be a place where it's safe to fail, to grow, and to be fully human.
Amen.

Jesus and the Invitation to Surrender

The world says: *Try harder. Be better. Prove your worth.* Jesus says: *Come as you are. Lay it down. Rest in Me.*

Children who struggle with perfectionism often live in a state of spiritual tension — even if they don't have the words for it. They believe love must be earned. That acceptance is conditional. That mistakes disqualify them from favour. But Jesus never made people hustle for His love. He welcomed the loud and the messy. The uncertain. The ones who didn't get it right. Even His disciples — His *closest friends* — made mistake after mistake:

- Peter sliced a man's ear off in panic

- Thomas doubted

- James and John argued about who was most important

- And Peter, again... denied even knowing Jesus

Jesus didn't shame them. He called them back. Again and again. He restored Peter with a question, not a lecture:

> "Do you love me?" (John 21:15)

Not, "Did you do everything right?" Not, "Did you maintain your spiritual progress chart?" Just: *Do you love Me? Let's begin there.*

Surrender Is Not Giving Up — It's Giving Over

When we help our children surrender their need for perfection, we're not encouraging laziness or mediocrity. We're helping them to let go of fear-based striving, learn that grace is stronger than performance, and to trust that their identity is secure — even when they get it wrong. Jesus invites us to lay down our burdens, not because we've earned rest, but because He is rest.

> "Come to Me, all who are weary and burdened, and I will give you rest."
> — *Matthew 11:28*

That includes our children. And us, too. Letting go of perfectionism isn't just a mindset shift — it's a muscle that needs regular stretching. Some kids have spent years believing mistakes are dangerous. That mess equals failure. That "good enough" isn't *really* good enough. We can't snap them out of that. But we can walk them out — step by step. If your child has been tightly controlling their world for a long time, don't start by throwing them into a whirlwind of glitter and chaos. Start small. Let them practice being okay with things not being perfect — in safe, low-pressure ways. For example, decorate cupcakes *without a design plan,* use the "wrong" colour crayon on purpose, leave a small chore *unfinished* for an hour, wear mismatched socks together as a family challenge", or have a "mistake of the day" dinner chat — and celebrate it (what did you find 'trifficult' today?).

What you say — and how you say it — matters. Try these phrases:

- "Oops! I made a mistake. That's okay — I can fix it or laugh about it."

- "What matters most here? The fun, or the result?"

- "I love how you tried — even though it didn't go the way you planned."

- "Your peace is more important to me than perfect homework."

Focus Praise on Effort and Resilience

Instead of "You're so smart" or "You're perfect," say:

- "That was brave, to keep going even when it got tricky."

- "You showed patience when it didn't work the first time."

- "You're growing. That matters more than getting it right."

Practise Calm During Mistakes

Your child will learn from your response:

- Do you tense up when the milk spills?

- Do you sigh when they mess up a word?

- Do you try to fix things too quickly?

Sometimes, the most powerful message you can send is calm presence in the face of imperfection. Sit in the mess with them. Breathe slowly. Say, "We're okay. Mistakes live here, too."

Practices for Parents:

Praise That Heals, Not Pressures. Your child is already under enough pressure from their own perfectionist thoughts. These parenting practices can help reduce that pressure and increase emotional safety:

- Praise progress, not perfection

    "You're improving," not "You're the best."

- Model self-compassion

    "I made a mistake — that's part of learning."

- Celebrate mistakes as growth moments

    "What did we learn from that slip-up?"

- Avoid over-reassurance

"You'll be fine!" may sound dismissive. Try: "It's okay to feel nervous. Let's do this together."

- Create space for low-stakes creativity

  Do silly art. Cook without measuring. Let imperfection breathe.

- Speak identity apart from achievement

  "You're kind." "You're brave." "I love you because you're *you*."

> **🧠 PSYCH INSIGHT:**
> Praise that focuses solely on outcome (e.g., "You're so smart!" or "You're the best!") can trigger performance anxiety in kids prone to perfectionism. Their brain links identity with achievement, reinforcing the fear of failure. In contrast, praise that highlights effort, persistence, and emotional regulation helps develop a growth mindset, calming the brain's fear centres and supporting resilience.
>
> **📖 FAITH INSIGHT:**
> God never celebrates us for our performance. He affirms us for who we are — His beloved children. Even Jesus, before performing a single miracle, was declared: "This is my Son, whom I love; with Him I am well pleased." (Matthew 3:17)

We can echo that same truth to our children: *"I'm pleased with who you are — not what you do."*

Maybe you've just realised that your "easy" child is quietly exhausted. Maybe you've seen glimpses of worry hiding in the corners of achievement. Maybe you've caught yourself praising gold stars more than gentle bravery. This chapter isn't here to shame you. It's here to help you see — and to remind you that it's never too late to lighten the load. You don't have to fix your child. You just get to walk with them — away from fear, and toward grace. Ask yourself: What might shift if I made room for mistakes? How can I model rest, surrender, and self-compassion in my own life? Where has God already been whispering, *"Let go — I've got this."*

A Word Over You, Dear Parent

You are not your child's coach. You are not their critic. You are not the referee keeping score. You are their safe place. Their mirror of God's love. Their reminder that *they are already enough.* You don't have to have the perfect script. You don't need a parenting trophy. You just need open arms and a heart that says: "You don't have to get it right. You just have to let God hold you."

Even as you guide your child, God is guiding you. Let the glue stick be crooked. Let the spelling word be wrong. Let the story unfold with mess and mercy. You are not raising a performance. You are raising a person — and they are so deeply loved.

Chapter 7

The Body Keeps the Score (Even in Little Bodies)

Helping kids listen to, trust, and calm their anxious bodies

"My Tummy Hurts Again"

Zara was seven. Bright. Shy. A daydreamer with a soft spot for fairies and fuzzy socks. Her parents brought her to see me because she'd started getting tummy aches every morning before school. She wasn't being bullied. She liked her teacher. There was no big drama. But still — the tears at breakfast. The clutching of her stomach. The pleading: *"I don't feel good. Can I stay home?"* Her GP found nothing medically wrong. She wasn't faking. She wasn't being manipulative. Zara's body was simply sounding the alarm before her mind even knew why.

Anxiety Lives in the Body

Most people think of anxiety as something that happens in the mind — *"I'm nervous." "I'm scared." "What if?"* But for many kids, anxiety speaks first through the body: Tummy aches, headaches, nail biting, tense shoulders, restlessness, trouble sleeping, quick breathing, or needing the toilet *again.* Sometimes, they don't even have words for what's wrong — they just *don't feel right.* And that's because the body is doing exactly what God designed it to do: Respond to danger. The problem is when the alarm system gets stuck on — even when there's no real threat.

Bodies Are Sacred, Too

God made us embodied beings. Our emotions don't float above us like thought bubbles — they live inside us. David wrote, "My heart is in anguish... terror of death has fallen on me... my body trembles." (Psalm 55:4–5). Elijah ran from his fear and collapsed under a bush — not to talk, but to sleep. Jesus sweat drops of blood in the garden — His anxiety poured through His skin. When our children's bodies "act out," they're not being difficult. They're inviting us to listen more deeply.

Children often struggle to name anxiety directly, so their bodies speak for them. And because the brain and body are intimately connected, this distress is very real — even if there's no fever or virus. These symptoms aren't imagined. They're caused by the child's nervous system preparing for perceived danger — pumping adrenaline, tightening muscles, diverting blood flow, speeding up the heart.

The Body's Alarm System

When a child feels anxious, their body's fight-flight-freeze response kicks in — whether or not there's an actual danger. This ancient system is designed to protect us, but in modern life, it often overreacts to emotional threats. For example: A spelling test feels like a *threat to identity.* A sleepover feels like a *threat to safety.* A disappointed teacher feels like a *threat to connection.* And so, their body prepares as if it's facing a tiger... not a timed quiz or awkward group project.

What This Means for Us as Parents

It means that when your child complains of physical symptoms, your first response should be: "Thanks for telling me. Let's figure this out together." Instead of:

"You're fine, it's just in your head." Because to your child — it's in their whole body.

Parent Reflection:

- Have I noticed physical complaints in my child that tend to show up before school, bedtime, or social events?

- Have I ever brushed these off as "dramatic" or "attention-seeking," when perhaps they were cries for safety or support?

- Do I tend to look for physical fixes first (Panadol, hydration, rest), or do I stop to explore emotional undercurrents?

Take a moment to pray or journal:

Lord, give me eyes to see beneath the surface.
Let me hear the message behind my child's physical pain.
Help me respond with compassion, not dismissal.
Teach me to treat their bodies with respect — and their feelings with grace.
And give me wisdom to discern when to seek help,

when to offer calm, and when to simply hold them close.
Amen.

Why the Body Reacts Even When the Mind Doesn't Want It To

One of the hardest parts of anxiety is this: Your child doesn't choose it. They don't wake up thinking, *"Today I'll cry before school just to keep things interesting."* They don't want to feel shaky, teary, or nauseated. They're not trying to be difficult. They're being human — with a nervous system that's doing its job... just a little *too well.*

Meet the Amygdala: The Brain's Smoke Alarm

The amygdala is a tiny part of the brain that acts like a smoke alarm. Its job is to detect danger and launch a fast response — before we've even had time to think. When the amygdala senses something *might* be unsafe (even emotionally), it sends signals that:

- Speed up the heart rate

- Shut down digestion (hence tummy aches!)

- Tense muscles

- Shut off rational thinking (the prefrontal cortex takes a backseat)

All of this happens in a split second. The goal? Keep us alive. The problem? The amygdala doesn't know the difference between: a bear in the backyard, and a math test in the classroom. If your child has had stressful experiences, is naturally sensitive, or has been in environments where they felt unsafe — their brain may have learned to overfire.

"But I Don't Want to Be Like This"

Children often get frustrated with themselves. They want to go to the party. They want to perform in the school play. They want to sleep in their own bed. But their body says: "Nope. Not safe." And that can lead to even more distress — tears, shutdowns, self-criticism. That's why your calm, validating presence matters so much. When you say: "Your body's just trying to help you — but it's getting a little overprotective," you're helping your child move from shame to *understanding.*

The amygdala — your child's internal alarm system — is essential for survival. It's beautifully fast, but not very smart. It reacts quickly, not accurately. This means children with anxiety may have amygdalas that are overactive, sounding the alarm even when there's no real threat. This isn't bad wiring. It's protective wiring — just a bit too sensitive. Through gentle exposure, safety cues, and co-regulation, the brain can learn: *"I'm safe now. I don't need to panic."*

God made our bodies to protect us. Fear isn't sin — it's a signal. But God never meant for us to live under constant alarm. That's why He offers rest for our minds *and* our bodies.

"You will lie down and sleep in peace, for the Lord makes you dwell in safety." — Psalm 4:8

Our job as parents isn't to eliminate every fear, but to help our child feel held — by us, and by God.

Tummy Aches, Tears, and Tension: What Anxiety Feels Like Physically

Ask a child how they feel when they're anxious, and you'll get some curious — and often very accurate — descriptions:

> "Like my legs are buzzing."
> "Like a bowling ball is in my tummy."
> "Like a balloon is stuck in my throat."
> "Like I can't breathe properly, but I still am."
> "Like my brain is racing and can't catch up."

These aren't dramatic metaphors. They're real bodily experiences, caused by a surge of stress hormones like cortisol and adrenaline. Common physical sensations of anxiety may present as; tight chest or shallow breathing, butterflies in the stomach, sweaty palms, lump in the throat, shaky hands or knees, racing heartbeat, dry mouth, and muscle aches or jaw clenching. These physical symptoms can make kids think: "Something is wrong with me." "I must be sick." "This means I shouldn't go." "I'll never feel okay again." That's why it's so important to name these sensations, explain what's happening, and offer tools to ride the wave. Because anxiety in the body feels scary — until a child understands it, and knows they're not alone.

Is It Anxiety... or Something Else?

One of the hardest parts about parenting an anxious child is this question:

> "How do I know if this tummy ache is anxiety — or a real problem?"

The answer is: It could be both. Anxiety causes real physical symptoms. But kids also get colds. They get constipated. They get the flu, sore throats, and the occasional weird rash that no one can explain but somehow resolves on its own. So how do you know? When in doubt, you can run through a few discernment questions like the following example;

1. When and where do the symptoms show up?

    - Does your child's tummy only hurt before school or church, but not during a movie night or playdate?

    - Are headaches appearing mostly before performance-related situations?

2. *Timing is a big clue. Anxiety symptoms are often situational.*

3. Do symptoms shift or ease with distraction or comfort?

    o If your child seems fine after staying home, or perks up after a cuddle and some play — it might be emotional.

    o Physical illness tends to persist regardless of the environment.

4. Is this part of a pattern?

    o Track frequency. If symptoms cluster around transitions or separations, you may be seeing a stress response.

5. *Look for consistency across contexts and triggers.*

Always trust your gut. If something feels off — get it checked. Ruling out medical issues can bring peace of mind *and* help you know what you're really dealing with. See a GP if:

- Your child has ongoing, unexplained symptoms

- They lose weight, energy, or interest in food

- They're avoiding daily life more and more

- You're just... not sure

Doctors and therapists can work together. This isn't either/or — it's whole-child care. When in doubt, use this with your child: "Let's look after your body and your feelings — both matter. If it's your tummy or your thoughts causing this, we'll figure it out together." This tells your child: You believe them. You're not brushing it off. You're on their team, whatever it turns out to be.

God Made Bodies — And They're Talking to Us

Helping kids listen to their body with kindness, not fear. In a world that often teaches children to ignore or override their feelings — "toughen up," "get over it," "don't be silly" — anxiety can become even more confusing. But Scripture teaches something different. Over and over, we see people in the Bible respond to emotion with their bodies:

- David weeps and trembles in the Psalms

- Elijah runs, collapses, and sleeps under the broom tree

- Jeremiah feels like his bones are on fire

- Jesus withdraws, sweats, kneels, and cries

- Paul talks about being afflicted in both body and mind

These aren't overreactions. They're honest, holy expressions of being fully human. God made our bodies with emotions wired in. Not to be dismissed — but to be listened to. When a child feels anxious in their body, our job isn't to say, *"Ignore it."* It's to say: "Let's listen together and figure out what your body is trying to tell us." You might try:

- "What do you feel in your body right now?"

- "If your tummy could talk, what would it say?"

- "Where in your body does your worry go?"

- "Let's check in with our shoulders and see if they need to relax."

This builds what psychologists call interoception — the skill of noticing internal signals — and helps your child separate *sensation from danger.* They learn: *"I can have a weird feeling… and still be okay."*

Interoception is your brain's ability to notice signals from your body — hunger, thirst, fatigue, tension, butterflies in the tummy. It's like an internal dashboard. Children with anxiety often misinterpret these signals as danger. A tight chest feels like something terrible is about to happen. A nervous tummy feels like an emergency. But by helping kids tune in to their bodies *without fear*, we increase emotional intelligence and resilience. We teach them that physical sensations are messengers, not enemies.

In Psalm 139:14, David writes *"I praise you because I am fearfully and wonderfully made."* That includes the *gut feelings*, the racing heart, and the shaky knees.
 God doesn't ask us to ignore our bodies — He calls us to bring our whole selves to Him. Jesus never healed people's hearts without also touching their physical wounds.

Movement is Medicine

Sometimes, the most powerful thing we can do for an anxious child… is to get them moving. When anxiety is high, talking often doesn't work. Logic doesn't land.

But movement? It shifts the energy. It resets the body. It clears space in the nervous system so the child can access calm again. When the body goes into fight-flight-freeze mode, adrenaline and cortisol flood the system. Muscles tighten. Breathing quickens. Energy builds up.

Movement allows that energy to be burned off in a safe and productive way — without shame, meltdown, or shutdown. It also helps reconnect the mind to the body, reset breathing and heart rate, boost feel-good chemicals like serotonin and dopamine, and distract from spirals and bring the child into the present moment.

Kid-Friendly Movement Tools

These can be done at home, school, church — anywhere:

- "Animal walks" (crab, bear, frog, snake)
- Wall pushes or chair dips
- Jumping jacks or trampoline breaks
- Stretching or yoga poses

- Carrying something heavy (a "helping job" around the house!)

- Slow, rhythmic swinging or rocking

- Dancing to silly music

- Running a lap or climbing playground equipment

- Playing with resistance bands or fidget toys

Even a 3-minute movement break can shift the emotional tone of the moment.

Parent Prompt:

- Have I ever felt frozen in anxiety myself — knowing that movement would help, but feeling too overwhelmed to begin?

- How might my child be experiencing that same inner tension, without the words to explain it?

When your child is in a low-energy anxious state (shut down, withdrawn, collapsed posture), movement can feel impossible — or even annoying. Instead of saying, *"You just need to move your body!"*, try these gentle bridges:

Offer Co-Movement:

> "I'm going to stretch my arms like a sleepy cat. Want to copy me?"
> "Let's shake our fingers out together — ready, 3…2…1…"
> "Will you help me carry this basket? I need your strong muscles!"

Use Micro-Movements. Start with very small, simple movements like, wiggle toes, rub hands together, tap fingers, or sway side to side while sitting. Pair with Comfort. Movement is more tolerable when paired with safety. Some examples of this include rocking together in a chair, walk while holding hands, or push palms together like a "calm high-five". Give Control Back. "I wonder if your body would like to move just a *little* bit — we can stop anytime." Your child isn't being lazy. They're likely overwhelmed, flooded, or protecting themselves the best way they know how. Trust the process. Connection is still the priority. Movement will follow when safety leads.

Breath, Laughter, Stretching, and Rest

When a child is anxious, it's tempting to talk them through it:

"Calm down."
"You're okay."
"It's not a big deal."
"Just take deep breaths."

But here's the truth: an anxious brain can't always process words. Especially when the body is tense and the nervous system is in high alert. That's why *doing* is often more powerful than *talking*. Let's explore four gentle tools that speak straight to the body:

Breath: Resetting from the Inside Out

Breath is one of the fastest ways to signal to the nervous system: *"We're safe now."* But not all kids like traditional deep breathing.

Try:

- Breathing with props (blow bubbles, pinwheels, dandelions)

- "Smell the flower, blow the candle" (inhale slowly, exhale gently)

- Box breathing with fingers (trace a square with your hand — breathe in, hold, out, hold)

- Breathing together on your lap or beside them — no words needed

Bonus: Whisper a verse on the exhale, like "Peace be still" or "God is near."

Laughter: God's Built-In Stress Release

Laughter releases dopamine, lowers cortisol, and helps the brain *reset* after stress. Even a forced giggle can snowball into a real laugh. It's science — and it's sacred. Bring on:

- Silly voices and accents

- Dad jokes, bad jokes, and made-up jokes

- Family dance-offs

- Ridiculous "draw a cat with your eyes closed" games

- Bible Mad Libs (yes, it's a thing!)

- The banana-on-the-head method (self-explanatory… and surprisingly effective)

Laughter doesn't dismiss emotion. It creates safety so those big emotions don't feel so heavy.

Jax was nine years old and wound so tight he made the Energizer Bunny look chill. He worried about everything — his school shoes being tied evenly, his spelling test scores, whether the fire alarm would go off *again* during assembly. His mum said he'd been anxious "since the womb" — but lately, even getting ready for school involved tears, tics, and tummy aches. One day during our session, I tried something different. I handed him a banana and asked him — completely straight-faced — to balance it on his head and tell me about his worst subject. He blinked at me. Then he giggled. And something softened in his shoulders. We spent the next ten minutes making banana hats, drawing mustaches on post-it notes, and turning my office into the most unproductive comedy sketch known to mankind.

Did it fix his anxiety? No. But that day, Jax learned that even when your body feels tight and your brain is racing, there is still space — *just enough space* — for joy. And laughter? It turns that sliver of space into a doorway for peace. But Is Laughter Biblical? Yes.

Deeply. The Bible speaks of joy over 200 times. Not forced happiness. Not spiritual fakery. But real, soul-deep gladness — often in the middle of suffering.

> "A cheerful heart is good medicine." — *Proverbs 17:22*
> "He will yet fill your mouth with laughter." — *Job 8:21*
> "We were like those who dream. Then our mouth was filled with laughter, and our tongue with shouts of joy." — *Psalm 126:1–2*

Jesus didn't shy away from emotion — and while the Gospels don't describe Him laughing, we know He was often in the company of children. Children who fidgeted. Children who joked. Children who got the giggles during synagogue. Children He *welcomed*. Laughter doesn't mock suffering — it reminds us we are *not* our suffering.

If your child is anxious, joy might feel out of reach. But it doesn't have to be earned. You don't need perfect circumstances to make room for it. You can build giggle breaks into the bedtime routine, keep a "laugh log" and share it at dinner, watch a silly video together before school, and let yourself laugh, even on hard days. When your child sees you laugh, they learn something crucial: *"We can feel scared, and still smile."* *"Our family makes room for joy — even in the mess."*

I once worked with a child at school who was struggling with overwhelming anxiety and emotional shutdowns. We were supposed to be doing something structured that day — a workbook, I think — but when we walked past the resource room, something unexpected happened. There was a bucket of forgotten balls. Ping pong balls, handballs, those weird little super-bouncy ones that seem to ricochet off gravity. And nearby? A stage with a perfect flight of wide steps.

So, we did what anyone would do: We invented the Great Ball Olympics. The rules were simple (and made up on the spot):

- Choose your champion ball

- See who can bounce it down the stairs with the most flair

- Bonus points if it lands in a specific "target zone"

- Extra bonus points if it makes us laugh

We ran. We threw. We belly-laughed. We invented ridiculous backstories for the balls and declared underdog victories with dramatic flair. At one point, we were both crying laughing as the world's tiniest ball did the world's worst bounce and just *plopped* down one step. What was happening neurologically? Movement. Regulation. Connection. Safe sensory input. A release of energy that had been locked in his little body for too long. But what we both remember most? The joy. In that moment, anxiety didn't have the last word. Play did.

You don't always need the "right" tool or a perfect plan. Sometimes, what your child needs is already in the room. A moment of permission — to move, to laugh, to forget the weight for a while. A moment where their body says: *"I feel good here."* And for a child with anxiety, that's not just fun. That's healing.

Stretching: Loosening Anxiety's Grip

Anxious bodies are tight — shoulders hunched, fists clenched, jaws locked. Stretching helps *open* the body, creating space for breath, presence, and peace. Try: pretend animal stretches (lazy lion, stretching cat, soaring eagle), reaching up and flopping down like a rag doll, yoga poses for kids — or just you, as they copy, or slow shoulder rolls, neck tilts, and toe wiggling. You don't need a perfect routine — just a few moments of *slowness and softness.*

Rest: Sometimes, the Answer is Stillness

Not every big feeling needs to be solved. Sometimes your child just needs permission to rest. Try: cuddling on the couch under a blanket, lying on the floor together with a hand on their back, gentle music or a quiet story, a whispered prayer of peace, a break from noise, light, or stimulation. Rest isn't giving up. It's letting the body reset, so the heart can try again later.

Joyful movement and laughter are not just pleasant — they are powerful tools for nervous system regulation. Laughter activates the parasympathetic nervous system, which helps the body shift out of fight-or-flight and into rest-and-digest mode. When a child laughs while moving their body, it signals: "I'm safe. I belong. I can relax." Even more than structured therapy exercises, spontaneous play that includes *joy* and *connection* offers deep healing — especially for anxious children who often live in hypervigilance.

God doesn't just tolerate laughter — He delights in it. And when we laugh with our children, we reflect His heart: A God who meets us in fear and leads us into freedom.

> 🧠 **PSYCH INSIGHT:**
> Joyful movement and laughter help calm the nervous system. They tell the body it's safe, shifting it out of stress mode. For anxious children, playful moments of connection can be even more healing than formal therapy — offering rest, trust, and relief from constant alertness.
>
> 📖 **FAITH INSIGHT:**
> Scripture paints a picture of joy as a holy response to being held by God:
> "The joy of the Lord is your strength." — Nehemiah 8:10
> "You have turned my mourning into dancing." — Psalm 30:11

Maybe you've seen it: the tummy aches, the clenched jaw, the sudden toilet dashes. Maybe your child's body seems to carry the weight of emotions they can't name. This chapter isn't about solving it all. It's about listening to the language your child's body speaks — and responding with curiosity, not correction. You don't have to diagnose every symptom. You don't need a perfect response every time. But when you say: *"Your body matters. I'm listening."* You're giving your child something anxiety can't take away: A sense of safety that lives in their skin.

A Word Over You, Dear Parent

You are not imagining it. You are not overreacting. You are not weak for crying when your child cries, or for cancelling plans again because they "don't feel good." You are showing up — again and again — in the quiet aches and long nights. And that matters.

God sees the way you hold your child's hand when their body shakes. He sees how you kneel beside them in waiting rooms and bathrooms and school corridors. He sees your exhaustion. And He calls you: faithful. Your child's body is fearfully and wonderfully made. And so is yours. Rest your shoulders. Stretch your arms. Let yourself laugh. Let God carry the tension you weren't meant to hold. He made your child's body and He holds their story. And He's not done yet.

Chapter 8

You're Not the Fixer (And That's a Good Thing)

Embracing your role as a guide, not a saviour

Chapter Purpose:

To free parents from the pressure of having all the answers, and guide them toward trust — in the process, in their child's growth, and most importantly, in God. This chapter is about:

- Relieving the "rescuer pressure" many parents carry

- Teaching the difference between *supporting* and *solving*

- Helping parents build emotional scaffolding without over-functioning

- Encouraging spiritual surrender over performance

- Showing how grace, not control, leads to true resilience

The Heavy Basket

"I just want to get it right."

That's what Claire said through tears, sitting across from me in a counselling session. She was exhausted. Her eight-year-old son, Sam, had developed a fear of vomiting that had turned family life upside down — no sharing food, no eating out, no birthday parties, no school camp. Claire had done everything "right": read the books, followed the therapy plan, kept the home spotless, sanitised the school lunchbox three times a week. And still... Sam was struggling. She looked at me and whispered: "If I can't fix this, what does that say about me?" It's a question most parents don't say out loud — but many carry quietly in their hearts.

Whether it's anxiety, sadness, sensory issues, tantrums, friendship drama, or bedtime fears — we want to make it stop. We want to solve it, smooth it, silence it. Not because we're controlling. Because we love them. Because we don't want them to suffer. Because *somewhere deep down* we've bought the lie: *"If I do everything right, they'll be okay."* But here's what I tell parents like Claire: You are not the Saviour. You are not the Healer. You are not the Fixer. You are the parent — a tender, trusted guide. And your child doesn't need a perfect fixer. They need a present one.

Parent Reflection:

Take a breath. Put your hand on your chest — right where the pressure tends to sit.
 Now ask yourself:

- Have I been believing that my child's wellbeing rests solely on me?

- Have I been treating every outburst, ache, or worry as something to fix, rather than something to walk through together?

- Have I been measuring my worth as a parent by my child's emotional state?

What would it feel like to hand that weight back to God? What if your child doesn't need a fixer... but a faithful presence?

God, I confess I've been holding more than I'm meant to.
Help me release what isn't mine to carry.
Help me hold what is mine — with tenderness and trust.
Teach me to walk with my child, not in front of them trying to clear every path.
And remind me that You are the one who saves — not me.
Amen.

The weight we weren't' meant to carry

Somewhere between the baby books and the big feelings, many of us picked up a belief that sounds noble... but becomes unbearable: *"If I love my child enough, I'll protect them from pain."* And at first, it feels right. We rock them when they cry. We pick them up when they fall. We soften the world where we can. That's what good parents do — we *care.* But as children grow, so do their worries, their wounds, their "what ifs."

And love — the same love that made us so devoted — can quietly morph into something else: hypervigilance, control, guilt, panic, exhaustion. We begin to believe that we must fix every anxious thought, preempt every meltdown, and get it *right* every single time. And when our child is still struggling, we feel like failures.

Anxious kids often have very emotionally attuned parents. That's not a flaw — that's a strength. It means you *notice* the changes, the moods, the subtle signs others might miss. But it can also mean you carry more pressure. You try harder. You learn more. You blame yourself more quickly. And here's the quiet danger: When we make our child's stability the measure of our success, we unintentionally tie our *identity* to their performance. If they're okay, I'm okay. If they're not, I must be doing something wrong. That's an impossible load.

It's not what God asks of us. It's not what your child needs. And it's not sustainable. God never asked you to be the perfect protector. He asked you to be faithful — to love, to guide, to trust Him with the outcomes. Because even the best parenting doesn't prevent suffering. But faithful parenting creates a space where suffering doesn't have to be faced alone.

If you're the parent of an anxious child, it's easy to fall into "fix-it" mode. You hear the worry, you feel the tension rise — and before you know it, you're solving:

- "You'll be fine!"

- "Just don't think about it."

- "Let me handle that."

- "Okay, we'll stay home."

- "I'll call the teacher."

And in the moment, it works — kind of. The tears stop. The meltdown ends. The situation gets smoothed. But here's the problem: fixing teaches dependence. Guiding teaches resilience.

Fixing Says:

- "You can't handle this without me."

- "Your feelings are too much."

- "I'm anxious about your anxiety."

It's often fear in disguise. Loving fear, protective fear — but fear all the same.

Guiding Says:

- "I believe you can do hard things — and I'll walk beside you."

- "Let's take one small step together."

- "This feels scary, but you are safe, and not alone."

Guiding doesn't ignore anxiety. It acknowledges it *and* invites growth.

In real life, guiding might look like;

- **Instead of** removing the problem...
  Prepare for it together.

- **Instead of** over-reassuring...
  Help them sit with discomfort.

- **Instead of** solving it all...
  Support their next brave step.

"It's okay to be scared — we can feel scared and do it anyway." "Let's talk through what might happen and how we'll handle it." "Even if you feel nervous, you're not alone — I'm with you, and God is too."

Ellie was a bright, kind 10-year-old with a soft heart and big fears — especially about getting sick. She avoided water fountains, touched classroom surfaces with her sleeves, and had memorised every ingredient in her lunchbox in case something could make her unwell. At first, her mum (let's call her Lisa) did what most parents would do — she reassured: "You're not going to get sick." "That lunch is fine." "Just try to stop thinking about it." But the questions didn't stop. Every day before school: "What if someone coughs on me?" "What if the bread has mould?" "What if I throw up at assembly?"

Lisa, exhausted and unsure, eventually gave in to avoidance routines:

- She packed separate lunch containers "just in case."

- She let Ellie stay home on assembly days.

- She stopped insisting on school altogether when the anxiety peaked.

She loved her daughter. She was doing everything she could to protect her. But Ellie wasn't getting better. She was getting more afraid. Over-accommodation teaches the brain: "This situation really is dangerous." "You can't handle it without someone rescuing you." "Avoidance = safety." And while avoidance brings short-term relief, it fuels long-term fear. It confirms the child's worst belief: *"I can't cope."*

Sometimes, our child's anxiety triggers our own anxiety. It sounds like this; "I can't bear to see them upset." "What if they hate me?" "What if I make it worse?" "What if I push too hard and damage them forever?" These are real fears. They're tender. And they deserve compassion. But they don't make good decision-makers. We have to pause and ask: *"Am I helping them grow? Or am I helping them escape?"*

Saying "no" to the fear — gently, firmly — is an act of love. "I know this feels scary. But we are still going to school today." "I'll be right here when it's over." "We're going to eat this meal together, even if it's tricky." Boundaries say: *"I believe in you. You are capable. We can face this together."* That belief — more than any fix — is what helps an anxious child grow.

Surrendering Control Doesn't Mean Surrendering Care

One of the hardest truths to accept as a parent of an anxious child is this: You can't control how your child feels. You can't control how their brain processes fear. You can't control how long it takes to heal. But you *can* control how you show up. You can be: Calm when their body is in chaos, soft when their tone is sharp, present when their fear pushes you away, consistent when everything else feels unpredictable.

That is not giving up. That is giving space for God to do what only He can do.

Control says; "If I hold tight enough, nothing bad will happen." "If I let go, I'm failing." "If I don't fix this, I don't love enough."

But care says: "I'll stay with you through this." "I'll do my part, and trust God with the rest." "You are not alone, even when I can't make it better."

Letting go of control is *not* the same as letting go of your child. In fact, surrender makes more room for love to breathe.

Surrender isn't passive. It's active trust. It looks like praying for your child's heart *instead of* rehearsing every worst-case scenario, taking breaks when you're overwhelmed, knowing your child's needs don't have to erase your own, allowing natural consequences instead of over-correcting everything, saying, "I don't know, but I trust that we'll find a way through this", and letting your child try, fail, and learn — even when it's hard to watch. Surrender says: *"God, I'm here to walk beside them. But I trust You to hold the map."*

Throughout Scripture, we meet parents who didn't get to control the outcome — but chose to trust God anyway.

Take Jochebed, the mother of Moses. Her baby was born into a world of danger, where Pharaoh had ordered all Hebrew boys to be killed. She hid him for as long as she could, but there came a day when she had to do the unthinkable: place him in a basket and release him into the Nile. That wasn't an act of helplessness. It was an act of courage — the kind of surrender that says, *I've done all I can. Now I entrust him to God.* And God did not abandon that floating basket. He guided it straight to Pharaoh's daughter and used Jochebed's brave release to raise up a leader who would one day part seas.

Then there's Mary, the mother of Jesus. She couldn't shield Him from hardship. She couldn't stop the betrayal, the injustice, the cross. But she stayed. She was there when He stayed behind in the temple at age twelve, when the world misunderstood His mission, when the crowds turned against Him. She couldn't fix what was coming — but she didn't leave. Her presence was not powerless. It was faithful. And that faithfulness became part of Jesus' story.

And let's not forget Joseph, the earthly father of Jesus. He had plans — a quiet life, a respectable marriage. But God interrupted those plans with something far more complicated. Joseph listened. He adapted. He protected Mary and Jesus, moved towns when danger arose, lived in obscurity. He wasn't loud. He wasn't flashy. But he was obedient. And his steady "yes" made room for the Saviour to grow up in safety.

None of these parents were in control. But all of them were available, responsive, and willing to trust God with the outcome. And that's the invitation to us, too. You can be a faithful parent... even if your child is struggling. You can surrender... and still be strong. You can stay near... even when you can't make it better. Because parenting, at its core, is not about perfection — it's about presence, trust, and courageous love.

The common thread here is these parents weren't flawless. But they were available, responsive, and willing to trust God with the outcome. They remind us: You can be a good parent... even if your child struggles. You can be faithful... even when you feel unsure. You can surrender... and still be strong.

Why Helicopter Parenting Increases Anxiety

Children develop emotional resilience by building a sense of competence — the belief that *"I can handle hard things."* When adults consistently step in to prevent distress, the child's brain doesn't get the opportunity to learn how to problem-solve, how to regulate emotions and how to recover from challenge.

In psychological terms, this reduces the development of autonomy — one of the three core needs for mental wellbeing. In short: *When we over-help, we under-trust.* Anxious children especially need gentle, consistent nudges to *try*, *struggle*, and *succeed* in small steps — not be rescued at every turn.

Even God doesn't helicopter parent us. He doesn't step in to fix every discomfort. He walks beside us, empowers us, and calls us **up** — not just in.

> "Do not fear, for I am with you… I will uphold you with my righteous right hand."
> — Isaiah 41:10

God doesn't take away the challenge — but He offers us presence, strength, and courage to grow through it. And that's our job too.

How Parental Anxiety Shapes the Emotional Climate

Children learn how to interpret the world not just through what we say — but through how we feel. They are wired to attune to our emotions. Even before they understand words, they are watching the way our shoulders tense when the phone rings, the edge in our voice when we say "Just wait a minute", the sigh when they spill their cereal, the panic when they cough. And they take it in as data: *"If Mum is worried, I should be worried."* *"If Dad is stressed, maybe this is my fault."* *"If this little thing upset them, I better stay small."*

If we are constantly scanning for danger, our children learn to do the same. A parent who is trying to be *very careful* can unintentionally create a home where spontaneity feels unsafe, or mistakes feel catastrophic, emotional expression is "too much", or new experience comes with a warning label. Even well-meant protection — "be careful," "don't touch that," "what if you get sick?" — teaches a child *"The world is dangerous. I need to be on guard."* Their nervous system mirrors yours. If you're on high alert, their little body learns to be, too.

If you are depleted, overwhelmed, or constantly stretched, even small interruptions (a tantrum, a spilt drink, another "what if" question) can feel like too much. In these moments, your child may interpret your reactions as: *"I'm a burden." "My needs are a problem." "I should stop asking for help." "I make things worse."*

That's not what you *meant*. But it might be what they *receive*. As a result children may internalise the stress. They try harder to manage on their own. Or they escalate their behaviour, trying to get your attention another way.

We all have moments of stress. We all sigh. We all say the wrong thing. This isn't about guilt. It's about gently noticing the emotional climate we carry — and how it shapes the environment our child lives in. Because children don't need perfect parents.

They need self-aware ones. Ones who can say: *"That wasn't your fault — I was having a hard moment." "It's okay to feel things. I'm learning too." "You are not too much."*

This awareness can actually reduce anxiety — for both you and your child. That's because when you begin to co-regulate your own emotional state, you change the atmosphere of your home. You model safety. You model grace.

Parent Prompt:

Pause for a moment. Take a breath. Place your hand over your heart, and ask yourself:

- What's the emotional "climate" in our home lately? Is it tense, tender, chaotic, calm?

- When my child is upset, what do I feel in my own body? Do I brace, rush, fix, sigh?

- What messages might my child be receiving — not from my words, but from my reactions?

Now gently ask:

- What would it feel like to respond *not from fear*, but from peace?

- What helps *me* feel grounded, so I can offer grounding to them?

God, help me notice the atmosphere I carry.
Help me respond to my child not out of panic or pressure, but out of presence.
Teach me to be a gentle thermostat — not a reactive thermometer.

Let peace begin in me, and ripple outward to the ones I love.
Amen.

You weren't meant to be the fixer. Not because you're inadequate, but because you were never supposed to carry it all. You can't control your child's path. You can't erase their anxiety. You can't think and feel and decide on their behalf. But you can stay close. You can learn to sit in the discomfort without panic. You can give space without withdrawing love. Letting go of control is not the same as letting go of your child. In fact, when you stop scrambling to solve everything, you free both of you to find what really heals: trust, courage, presence, and peace. Let this be the chapter where you set down the weight you were never meant to carry.

A Word Over You, Dear Parent:

You are allowed to breathe. You don't have to be five steps ahead. You don't have to have the perfect script. You don't have to rescue them every time. You're allowed to cry in the pantry. You're allowed to feel unsure. You're allowed to say, "I don't know," and mean it. Your faithfulness is not measured in control. It's found in presence — in sitting beside your child when fear is loud, in offering your calm when theirs has run out, in saying, "I'm here," even when you don't have the solution.

God is the one who saves. But He's trusted you with something sacred: to walk with, not in front of, this child of His. May you trade fixing for faith. May you swap panic for peace. May you learn to rest in the truth that God's grace is enough — for you, and for your child. And may you know, in the deepest part of you, that you're not doing this alone.

Chapter 9

Let's Figure This Out Together

Chapter Purpose:

To empower parents to guide their child through anxiety and adversity using connection-based communication and practical thinking tools — without taking over or dismissing emotions. This chapter explores how to "coach" rather than command, and helps children develop confidence in their own capacity to handle challenges.

"I Don't Know What to Do!"

Noah stood at the top of the stairs in his socks and pyjamas, holding his stuffed frog and trying not to cry. He was seven. He'd been excited all week about his sleepover at Nana and Pop's house. They had promised pancakes for breakfast and let him stay up late to play Uno. But now it was bedtime — and he was frozen. "I don't know what to do," he said, voice trembling.

It wasn't the house. It wasn't his grandparents. It was the thought of something *going wrong* — a tummy ache, a nightmare, a mosquito in the room — and Mum not being there. His Nana tried to reassure. His Pop offered a joke. But the tears welled up anyway.

That's when his Mum, who had just arrived to drop off his overnight bag, knelt beside him. She didn't say, *"You're fine."* She didn't say, *"Don't be silly — it's just one night."* She didn't say, *"Come on, stop crying. Everyone's watching."* She said, *"Okay buddy, this feels hard. Let's figure it out together."*

And that changed everything. It wasn't about whether Noah stayed or went home that night. It wasn't about pancakes or bravery or whether his big sister had done sleepovers earlier. It was about safety and connection. And the invitation to approach a scary situation *with someone*, not *for someone*.

When anxiety hits, children often feel cornered. Their world shrinks. Their thoughts spiral. Their body gets flooded. And logic leaves the room. What they need isn't a solution thrown at them — it's a lifeline handed to them. "Let's figure it out together" is one of the most powerful phrases you can offer an anxious child. It says: *You don't have to face this alone. I won't force you through it, but I won't walk away either. We can think this through, one step at a time.* This chapter is about how to do that — how to become your child's thinking partner, not their pressure coach. It's not about perfect answers. It's about faithful presence, emotional scaffolding, and equipping your child to learn that they are capable, loved, and never alone — no matter what they're facing.

Noah's mum sat down on the stairs beside him, legs folded like she wasn't in a rush. Noah sniffled and leaned against her. She wrapped an arm around him and said quietly, "Okay... so it feels hard right now. You were excited, but now your tummy's doing somersaults." He nodded, face still buried. "Can you tell me what's bothering you the most? No wrong answers." Noah hesitated. Then whispered, "What if I throw up and you're not here?" His mum took a slow breath and stayed steady. "Ah, that's a really scary 'what if'. I get it. That would be awful. So let's figure out what we can do, just in case that happens. Not because we think it *will*, but because we know you'll feel better if you have a plan." Noah peeked up, curious through the fog of worry. "Like a plan for if I'm sick?" "Exactly. First — who would help you if something didn't feel right?"

"Nana."

"Yep. And do you think she'd be okay cleaning up and looking after you?"

"...She used to be a nurse."

"So I'd say she's pretty qualified," she smiled. "And I've already told her your bedtime meds are packed and where to find clean jammies. So you don't even have to say much — just come find her, and she'll take care of the rest." Noah was quiet again. "And you'll come tomorrow?"

"First thing. You'll probably still be eating pancakes." A tiny smile. A flicker of relief. "Okay. But can I sleep with my frog *and* the blanket from home?"

"Absolutely. And let's leave a note in your backpack that says: *'You are brave and safe and Nana knows what to do.'* Want to write it together?" Noah nodded. He still felt a little nervous. But he also felt prepared. Heard. Supported. Like this wasn't a test of courage — it was a learning moment, and he didn't have to pass it alone.

That's what collaborative problem-solving looks like. Not minimising. Not fixing. Just showing up — emotionally regulated, gently curious, and ready to think side-by-side. This story shows us what so many of the principles in this book are all about: not avoiding the fear, but approaching it with gentle curiosity and connection. Noah's mum didn't try to convince him his fear was silly, and she didn't swoop in to take it away.

Instead, she co-regulated first — offering presence and calm — and then invited him into a practical conversation where he could access his thinking brain again. She gave his fear a voice, gave his body a break, and gave his heart a plan. That's not over-accommodation. That's empowerment. And for an anxious child, that's the kind of moment that builds real courage — not because the fear was erased, but because they learned: *I can feel afraid and still move forward, especially when I have someone who sees me and helps me think it through.*

If you've ever tried to reason with your child in the middle of a meltdown, you already know: it doesn't work. That's not because your child is being difficult or disrespectful. It's because when anxiety spikes, the brain shifts gears — and logic gets temporarily unplugged. In the world of brain science, this is called amygdala hijack.

The brain's alarm system (the amygdala) senses threat and takes over — sending signals to the body to prepare for fight, flight, or freeze. Heart rate rises. Muscles tense. Breathing quickens. Thinking shuts down. You can't reason your way out of a fear response. You have to calm the body *before* the mind can process anything. This is why kids who seem "fine" one moment can't answer simple questions the next. It's not that they won't — it's that they can't. Their brain has gone into survival mode.

First Calm, Then Think

This is where many parents (understandably) get stuck. They try to help by jumping straight to logic: "It's not that big a deal." "You're not even sick." "There's nothing to worry about." "We talked about this already." "You're being irrational." But anxiety doesn't need facts first — it needs safety. Only once the nervous system has de-escalated can the child access the "thinking brain" again — the prefrontal cortex — which is responsible for decision-making, problem-solving, and self-reflection. The best thing you can do when your child is overwhelmed is to get low, get calm, and connect: "I can see this feels big. I'm here." "Let's take a moment to breathe together." "You don't have to figure it out right now. Let's settle first." These are the tools of co-regulation. They're not solutions — they're the bridge to solutions. When the emotional floodwaters recede, your child will be able to think again. And that's when the real magic can begin: not in pushing them forward, but in gently inviting them to explore what's possible... together.

Neuroscience teaches us that when the brain senses danger — even emotional danger — it prioritises survival over reasoning. That's why your child can't absorb your helpful words in the middle of a panic. Their brain isn't being disobedient; it's being protective. But the part of the brain that helps them solve problems — the prefrontal cortex — only comes back online when they feel safe. This is why co-regulation matters so much. When you lower your tone, soften your face, slow your pace, and offer calm — you're not giving in. You're giving access. You're creating the conditions for thinking, learning, and problem-solving to return.

In Scripture, we see the same rhythm in the way God relates to us. He doesn't barge into our distress with demands. He draws near. He speaks softly. He waits for us to breathe.

> "He will not crush the weakest reed or put out a flickering candle." — *Isaiah 42:3 (NLT)*
> "Be still, and know that I am God." — *Psalm 46:10*

Before God teaches, He comforts. Before He redirects, He restores. He meets us in the fear — and then invites us into trust. That's your invitation too. Not to rush your child through distress, but to anchor them through it. To model that peace is not the absence of fear, but the presence of love — even in the chaos.

Connection First, Then Strategy

It's tempting, when your child is distressed, to leap into problem-solving. You want to fix it. Ease the discomfort. Explain your way out of it. But anxious children don't need information first — they need connection. Because only when a child feels seen, soothed, and supported can their brain shift from survival to strategy.

Think about how God responds to us when we're overwhelmed. He doesn't start with a lecture. He starts with presence. "Fear not, for I am with you." — *Isaiah 41:10*. He doesn't demand calm. He creates space for it. That's what you're doing too when you say: "I'm here. We'll figure this out." "Let's just take a moment. You don't have to have the answer yet." "It's okay to feel how you feel. Let's breathe together." You are regulating *with* your child — helping them settle enough to access their own capacity. It's not about being perfectly calm all the time. It's about being the safe place they can return to when their feelings feel too big.

Before you say *anything* to try to help your child "think it through," start with something like: "This feels hard right now." "I can see this is a lot." "Let's pause and sit together before we decide anything." Let them borrow your calm. Let them feel anchored. Then —

and only then — you can begin to explore the next step together.

When a child is anxious, it can feel like you're the only one thinking clearly. So we do what any caring parent would do — we jump into decision-making mode: "You don't have to go." "We'll call the teacher." "We'll cancel that thing." "I'll sort it out for you." And sometimes, yes, in the heat of the moment, *you do need to lead*. But when that becomes the default, we rob our children of something sacred: The chance to learn they are capable.

Collaborative problem-solving doesn't mean throwing your child in the deep end. It means sitting beside them at the edge of the water and saying: "Let's work this through together." You're not forcing. You're not fixing. You're partnering. Let's go back to Noah's sleepover story. His mum didn't say, "Stop crying." She didn't say, "We'll just go home." She said: "Let's figure out a plan — not because we think something will go wrong, but so you'll feel ready if it does." Together, they listed his "what if" fears. They identified helpers. They made a comfort kit. They created a script for asking Nana for help. They wrote a little note that reminded him: *You are brave and safe.* Noah didn't conquer anxiety that night. But he *moved forward anyway*. That's the heart of collaborative problem-solving — moving forward together even when fear is still in the room.

When you approach challenges this way, you're not just solving a problem. You're teaching your child that their voice matters and their fear isn't too much for you. They don't have to do it alone, and problems can be unpacked gently. They can try — and survive — even with nerves in their pocket. And over time, you'll see it: they start bringing their fears to you sooner. Because they've learned you won't judge, dismiss, or panic. You'll sit with them. Think with them. Walk beside them. That's what rewires anxiety into courage.

Teaching a Thinking Voice (When Anxiety is Loud)

Once a child has been calmed and co-regulated, there's an open window — a space where their thinking brain is back online and their body is no longer flooded with alarm signals. That's the moment we begin to build something powerful: an inner voice that helps them think clearly when anxiety speaks loudly. We all have an inner narrator. For anxious kids, that narrator is often bossed around by fear: *"What if something bad happens?"* *"What if I can't do it?"* *"I feel weird — I must be sick."* These thoughts feel real, and sometimes they're so automatic that the child doesn't even notice them happening. That's why it helps to give these thoughts a name — something playful and external like *The Worry Voice*, *Bossy Brain*, or *The What-If Monster*.

Then we introduce a new voice: one that's calm, wise, and rooted in truth. We might call this *The Brave Voice*, *The Helper Thought*, or *God's Whisper*. Worry Voice says: *"You're going to mess it up."* Brave Voice says: *"It's okay to be nervous. You can try anyway."* Worry Voice says: *"You have a tummy ache. You must be really sick."*

Brave Voice says: *"Tummies feel funny when we're anxious. Let's take a breath and see if it passes."* Worry Voice says: *"Don't even try — you'll fail."* Brave Voice says: *"Trying is how we learn. You don't have to be perfect."*

This isn't about toxic positivity or ignoring real emotions. It's about training the brain to slow down and examine thoughts instead of automatically believing them.

>
>
> 🧠 **PSYCH INSIGHT:**
> Cognitive Behavioural Therapy (CBT) calls this process cognitive restructuring — helping children identify unhelpful thoughts and replace them with balanced ones.
>
> 📖 **FAITH INSIGHT:**
> Scripture calls it renewing the mind:
> "Do not be conformed to this world, but be transformed by the renewal of your mind..." — Romans 12:2 and
> "Take every thought captive to make it obedient to Christ." — 2 Corinthians 10:5

God knows our thoughts shape our lives. And He invites us to walk in truth, not fear. Helping a child identify the lies anxiety tells and replace them with truth is both psychologically sound and spiritually rooted. This is exactly the concept we teach children in our unique children's online anxiety management program.

Building the Brave Voice: A Story in Practice

After the school concert, Ellie clutched her mum's hand and burst into tears. From the outside, everything had gone fine. She sang her part, smiled in the group bow, and didn't forget the actions. But now, in the quiet of the car, the storm broke loose.

"I was terrible," she whispered, tears tracking down her cheeks. "Everyone saw me mess up. I looked stupid. I shouldn't have even gone up." Her mum didn't argue. She didn't try to talk her out of the feelings. Instead, she pulled the car over and looked her daughter in the eye. "Sweetheart, I can see how big those feelings are. Let's just sit with them for a second." Ellie sniffled. Her breathing slowed a little. Her shoulders started to drop from her ears.

Then her mum asked gently, "Can I ask... what did the worry voice tell you up on that stage?" Ellie blinked, caught off guard. "Um... that I was going to ruin it."

"That's a mean voice," her mum said. "What else?"

"That I was off-key. And my hair looked dumb."

"Ugh, classic Worry Voice," her mum said, shaking her head playfully. "Mine says things like that to me sometimes, too." Ellie gave a half-laugh.

"But let's pretend there was another voice in your head — a helper voice. One that knows the truth, even when you feel nervous. What do you think *that* voice would've said?" Ellie was quiet for a moment.

"Maybe... that I practised a lot? And... no one else noticed if I messed up?"

"Exactly. Maybe it would say: *You were brave just to get up there. Everyone makes little mistakes, and you did your best.*" She gave a tiny nod. Her tears had stopped now. Her body was calm. And her brain was thinking again. Her mum reached back and gave her hand a squeeze. "Next time the worry voice tries to yell at you, remember you have another voice — a brave one. And I'll help you practise listening to it."

That's how we teach kids to manage their inner world. Not through lectures. Not by minimising. But by drawing the anxious thought into the light, giving it a name — and introducing a new voice that tells the truth in love.

Parent Reflection:

When your child hears the worry voice, what do they hear in yours? Do they hear panic... pressure... the need to "snap out of it"? Or do they hear something calm and grounded — a reminder that they're safe, loved, and not alone? Think about the voices in your own head, too. The ones that show up when you mess up, run late, lose your cool. What does your inner narrator say to you?

Now ask:
What would change if I let God's voice be louder?

He doesn't say, *"You're failing."*
He says, *"You are my child. I'm not going anywhere."*

You don't have to model perfect thinking. You just have to offer a better way — one steady enough that your child might start believing it too.

You are not your child's fixer. You are their guide. Their calm in the chaos. Their reminder that fear doesn't get the final word. Your child doesn't need you to erase the hard things. They need you to sit beside them in the swirl, and say, *"Let's figure this out together."* Because every time you do that — Every time you pause before reacting, stay calm when they can't, Help them untangle the worry instead of shut it down — You're building something deep and durable. Not just coping strategies. Not just resilience. You're building trust — in themselves, in you, and in a God who holds them through it all.

A Word Over You, Dear Parent:

You don't have to have all the answers. You don't have to silence the worry before bedtime. Or make the tears disappear with the perfect phrase. Or turn every anxious moment into a teachable one. What you *can* do — and what matters most — is stay near. Breathe slow. Offer safety. And speak the kind of truth that calms the heart and opens the mind. You can say, *"This is hard, and I'm here."* You can say, *"Let's make a plan."* You can say, *"God sees you, even now."*

And when your child starts to believe those things, You'll see it — Not all at once, but over time: Confidence growing. Courage blooming. And peace — the kind that surpasses understanding — settling softly over your home.

Chapter 10

When Life Throws Curveballs

Helping Kids Face Change, Uncertainty, and Loss with Faith and Flexibility

---

The Box in the Bedroom

Liam stood at his bedroom door, watching his dad pack the last box. His favourite Lego spaceship had already been carefully wrapped in newspaper. His posters were rolled. His bed was bare. They were moving. Not just to another street — but to another town. Away from his school, his neighbours, and the friends he rode bikes with every afternoon. The place he had always called "home." His mum crouched beside him and said, "This new house has a big gum tree out the front. You're going to love it." Liam didn't move. "What if I hate it?" he said quietly. "What if no one likes me?" "What if I never feel normal again?"

His questions weren't just about the house. They were about *loss* — and the fear of everything changing.

Children face curveballs more often than we realise. Some are big and obvious — like moving, divorce, illness, or grief. Others are quieter but still painful — like a cancelled event, a friend suddenly pulling away, or a teacher who leaves mid-term. And sometimes, it's not the event itself — it's the *fear* of what could happen: "What if Mum gets sick again?" "What if the dog runs away?" "What if the world isn't safe?"

When uncertainty enters a child's world, their nervous system lights up. Their need for control intensifies. Their anxious thoughts get louder and more persistent — trying to protect them from what they can't predict. That's where we come in. Not with perfect answers. But with presence. We don't erase the curveballs. We guide them through. With honesty, comfort and a faith that says: *Even when everything changes, God does not.*

The Trouble with "What Ifs"

Children don't always know how to say, *"I feel anxious about the future."*
Instead, they ask questions. Again and again. "What if there's a fire while I'm at school?" "What if my tummy

hurts during assembly?" "What if Grandma dies while we're away?" Sometimes they whisper these questions at bedtime, right as you're reaching for the light. Sometimes they ask them ten times in one day, trying to trap the future into giving them a guarantee. And sometimes, they don't ask at all — they just *refuse to go*. Refuse to try. Refuse to eat, or sleep, or speak. Because underneath the surface of the "what ifs" is a deep desire for one thing: certainty.

Children thrive in predictability. They look for patterns, routines, and familiar faces to help them feel anchored in the world. When life feels uncertain — when something unexpected happens, or even just threatens to — that sense of safety crumbles. The brain doesn't say, *"This is a new situation. Let's see how it goes."* It says, *"Danger. Prepare to panic."* Anxiety loves the unknown. And for a child, the unknown is enormous. It might be a new baby coming into the family. Or a friend who suddenly stops waving at school. Or a change in Dad's job that means everything else changes too. Their brains are still learning how to hold big feelings, how to imagine different outcomes, and how to trust what they can't control. And when those skills aren't fully developed yet — which is totally normal — uncertainty feels like standing in a dark room with no light switch. That's why your child might become clingier, more explosive, or strangely quiet when change is coming. They're not trying to be difficult. They're trying to get their feet back on solid ground.

Holding Space for Grief, Fear, and Disappointment

We don't often use the word "grief" to describe a child missing their old school or crying over a broken toy — but maybe we should. Grief isn't just about death. It's about *loss* in all its forms: lost routines, lost relationships, lost normal. And for children, those losses can feel just as overwhelming and disorienting as they do for adults. The temptation, as a parent, is to soften the blow as quickly as possible. We want to rescue, reassure, or redirect. We say things like: "You'll make new friends." "It's not that big a deal." "Let's focus on the positive." We do this with the best of intentions. We want to lift them out of sadness. We want them to feel better — quickly. But when we jump to solutions or silver linings too soon, our kids learn that their sadness is something to move past, not move *through*.

What they really need is for us to hold the space with them — not to fill it. To say: "Yeah… this really stinks." "It's okay to feel upset." "I'm right here with you." There's something deeply healing that happens when a child sees you not rushing to change their emotions, but simply making room for them. That's what helps them feel safe enough to process what's happening, rather than suppress it. And grief is not linear. One day your child may seem totally fine. The next, they're overwhelmed again by a wave of sadness, fear, or even anger. That's normal. That's grief doing its work. Instead of viewing their big emotions as setbacks, we can begin to see them as signs of a heart that's trying to make sense of change — and a parent who's willing to stay close while they do.

Your child's brain is beautifully designed to keep them safe. It scans the environment constantly for signs of danger — not just physical threats, but emotional ones too. And one of the things the brain dislikes most? Uncertainty.

When something unexpected happens — or might happen — the amygdala (the brain's smoke alarm) lights up. It sends signals to the nervous system: *Something's not right. Prepare to act.* That's when your child might cling, lash out, spiral into "what if" questions, or freeze altogether.

The tricky part is that the brain doesn't wait for *proof* of danger. It reacts to the *possibility* of danger. And for an anxious child, those possibilities can feel endless. Their body responds just like it would to a real emergency — heart pounding, stomach tight, thinking brain offline.

But here's the hope: Safety doesn't always come from having all the answers. It can also come from connection and trust.

When you calmly acknowledge their fears, offer comfort, and remain a steady presence, you're helping their nervous system reset. You're sending the message: *This might be hard, but we're not alone. We're safe together.* This is where faith becomes more than just belief — it becomes regulation.

Scripture doesn't promise a predictable life. But it *does* promise a present God.

> "God is our refuge and strength,
> an ever-present help in trouble.
> Therefore we will not fear…"
> — *Psalm 46:1–2*

When a child begins to understand that even in the unknown, God remains unshaken — their brain learns something beautiful: *I don't have to know everything. I just need to know who's with me.*

When Max's guinea pig, Pickles, died, the house got quiet in a new kind of way. Pickles had been part of the family for two years. Max fed her kale every morning, cleaned her cage (mostly), and whispered secrets into her fur when he felt lonely. So when he found her lying still one afternoon, everything in him seemed to drop. His parents offered gentle words: "She lived a good life." "We'll miss her." "You gave her so much love." But Max didn't want comfort yet. He needed to *feel it* — to cry, to be mad, to stare at the empty space in his room and say, "It's not fair." And so his mum sat beside him on the floor. Not rushing. Not fixing. Just being.

Later that week, they had a small backyard memorial. Max placed a stone near the garden with a hand-drawn picture of Pickles taped to it. They lit a candle. His dad read a short Psalm. Max prayed through tears: "Thank you for Pickles. I don't know why she died, but I know she's not alone now." That moment didn't erase the grief — but it gave it shape. It gave it language. It gave it honour.

Children need permission to grieve — not just the big losses, but the little ones too. The cancelled playdate. The goodbye to a teacher. The sibling who moves out. The innocence that slips away after a scary news story. And they need us to *model* what it means to grieve with hope. Not pretending everything is fine. Not rushing into "God has a plan." But saying honestly, *"This hurts. Let's talk to God about it."* Sometimes that means creating little rituals — writing letters, planting a tree, lighting a candle.

Sometimes it means naming feelings without needing to solve them. Sometimes it means admitting, *"I don't understand either. But God is still with us."* Grief and hope can hold hands. In fact, that's where faith shines brightest — in the tension between *what we've lost* and *what we still trust.*

Children are natural theologians. They ask the kinds of questions most adults avoid: "Why did God let this happen?" "Why didn't He stop it?" "Where was He when I was scared?" And as parents, these questions can rattle us. We want to give answers that comfort, but sometimes the simple answers feel… well, too simple. "Everything happens for a reason." "God won't give you more than you can handle." "Just have faith." But these phrases — while often well-meaning — can leave children feeling unseen or confused. If God only allows hard things for a reason, then does that mean He *wanted* them to suffer? If they still feel sad after praying, does that mean their faith isn't strong enough? This is why we must guide our children not just to a set of beliefs, but to a *relationship* with a God who is big enough to hold their questions — and tender enough to meet them in the middle of them.

A resilient theology doesn't shy away from mystery. It says: "I don't know why this happened… but I know God is with us." "I don't understand this… but I do know God sees you." "It's okay to cry. God doesn't expect you to be happy all the time." One mother shared how her daughter, after losing her grandfather, asked if it was okay to be angry at God. Instead of correcting her, she opened the Bible to the Psalms — and showed her David's honest words. "Why, Lord, do you stand far off?" "My tears have been my food day and night." "How long, O Lord?" They read those verses together, and the little girl whispered, "So... I'm not the only one?" That's theology at work — not in perfectly memorised answers, but in *companionship with a God who welcomes our emotion.*

We want our kids to know that faith isn't about never doubting, never crying, or never feeling disappointed. It's about knowing who to bring those feelings to. It's about discovering that even in the hardest moments, *God doesn't pull away — He draws near.*

Parent Reflection

Think back to a time when something unexpected disrupted your world. It might've been a move, a breakup, an illness, or a loss that still brings a quiet ache. Now ask yourself — what helped you through it? Was it someone's presence? A comforting routine?

A scripture or whispered prayer that reminded you God had not disappeared?

Our children don't need a pain-free life. They need tools. They need presence. They need a faith that's strong enough to lean on when everything else feels shaky. And they need to borrow *our* calm when their own is gone. You don't need all the answers. You just need to be willing to sit in the questions with them.

A Word Over You, Dear Parent

You will not be able to protect your child from every heartbreak. There will be curveballs, cancelled plans, sick days and unexpected goodbyes. Questions with no neat answers. But you are not powerless in those moments. You are the steady hand in the storm. The one who says, *"This hurts. I'm here. And God is, too."* You are the whisper that reminds them — grief is not the end of the story. Change is not the end of safety. And fear is not the voice that gets the final say. So stay close and keep pointing to the One who never changes. That is what makes a child resilient. Not the absence of hardship, but the presence of love through it.

Chapter 11

Planting Seeds for the Long Haul

Creating a Family Culture That Nurtures Emotional and Spiritual Resilience

---

Chapter Purpose:

To help parents integrate the key principles of this book into everyday life — not just in response to anxiety, but as part of the long-term emotional and spiritual formation of the home. This chapter encourages a shift from reactive to proactive parenting.

In the early years of parenting, I spent a lot of time hoping for *breakthroughs*. One good day, one deep conversation, one tearful prayer — surely that would be enough to turn the tide. Surely after that one moment, everything would click. Sometimes it did. Most of the time, it didn't. Most of the time, parenting felt more like watering a plant I couldn't see growing yet. That's when I started to shift how I thought about the work of raising an emotionally and spiritually healthy child. It wasn't about one-off victories — it was about cultivation. We were building something over time — like planting a garden. Some seeds sprouted quickly. Others took months. Some looked like they had died off altogether... only to surprise us with life when the conditions were just right. And like any good gardener, I realised my job wasn't to force fruit. It was to tend the soil, show up daily and pull a few weeds. To trust the process.

Parenting anxious or sensitive children requires exactly this kind of slow, faithful tending. You don't always get immediate results. You can say the same comforting phrase for weeks before it finally sticks. You might teach a breathing strategy that gets eye-rolls for a year — and then one day, your child uses it on their own without being asked. That's the work of planting seeds. Not dramatic. Not glamorous. But deeply sacred. Because what you're building isn't just coping skills — it's a whole family culture: one where emotions are understood, grace is abundant, and God's presence is part of everyday life.

Emotional safety isn't just a "strategy" we pull out in a crisis. It's a *culture* — something we build through rhythms, tone, presence, and even how we recover from hard moments. In families where anxiety tends to flare, it's easy to fall into patterns of reacting: the meltdown happens, the parent jumps in, the tools come out. But what if safety was woven into the day *before* the panic set in? What if your home had *layers of predictability* that your child could lean into — like emotional scaffolding?

That might look like:

- A few minutes each day for check-in conversations, even just while folding laundry or walking the dog.

- Using a common language to name emotions: "Looks like frustration just showed up. Want help with it?"

- Keeping calm-down tools somewhere visible — not as a punishment, but as a gift: "Hey, if you need your glitter jar or want a cuddle, they're right here."

- Saying "I'm sorry" as a parent — and modelling repair without shame.

- Praying together in the little things, not just the big ones: before an exam, after a fight, at bedtime, or even in the car on the way to school.

These small choices begin to teach a child: *This is a place where I can bring all of me.* Not just my good behaviour. Not just my best days. But the parts of me that feel uncertain, overwhelmed, or undone. It also teaches them something about God — that He isn't just present when we're polished. He's with us in the mess, too. When emotional safety becomes a lifestyle, not just a reaction, kids learn that emotions aren't emergencies. They're part of being human. They can feel big things, and those things will be welcomed, not punished. And over time, that changes the air in the home. It doesn't mean things are always peaceful — it means the *path back to peace* is well-worn.

The brain learns through repetition. Every time a child has a certain kind of experience — a soothing voice during distress, a gentle explanation instead of shame, a moment of connection instead of punishment — the brain lays down a track, like footprints in soft sand. Repeat the experience enough times, and those tracks become a pathway. The child's brain begins to expect safety. Begins to predict comfort. Begins to choose self-regulation because the pattern has been laid. That's the neuroscience of habit. But it's also the rhythm of *discipleship*.

In Deuteronomy 6, God tells His people to teach their children about His commands and character — not just once, but repeatedly, as part of daily life:

> "Talk about them when you sit at home and when you walk along the road,
> when you lie down and when you get up."
> — *Deuteronomy 6:7*

Repetition, in both faith and mental health, is not a sign of failure — it's how learning happens. So every time you kneel beside the bed and pray, every time you pause to breathe instead of react, every time you sit beside the meltdown and say, *"I'm here. We'll figure this out together"* — you're helping wire your child's brain for security. And you're anchoring their spirit in something unshakable. They may not remember every conversation. But their body will remember how it felt to be held, seen, and safe. And one day, when life throws its curveballs, those neural and spiritual pathways will rise to meet them — not with panic, but with peace.

What It Looks Like Over Time

When the Jennings family first came to see me, they described their household as "tense" and "always on edge." Their eight-year-old son, Josh, was having frequent meltdowns — especially before school — and their six-year-old daughter had started mimicking his outbursts, creating what they jokingly called "morning mayhem." Mum said she felt like a failure most days. Dad admitted he didn't know how to help without yelling. The house felt like a minefield. Everyone was bracing for the next explosion.

But they were open. Willing. Tired — but teachable. They didn't overhaul everything at once. Instead, they started small. The first step was to identify one moment in the day to focus on connection instead of correction: the drive to school. Instead of drilling the morning schedule or reacting to Josh's resistance, they began a new ritual. One parent would pray out loud — not long, just a sentence or two — and then ask, "Is there anything we can ask God to help with today?"

At first, Josh just shrugged. But eventually, he whispered things like, "Maths test," or "Don't want to get in trouble." And soon, his little sister began chiming in too. They started adding "calm down corners" in their bedrooms — not as a punishment, but as a retreat space. They put soft pillows, scripture cards, and a basket of sensory tools inside. They began using new phrases: "Let's take a break and come back to this." "Looks like your worry voice is talking — let's ask God to help quiet it." "We're on the same team."

It didn't stop the hard moments — not by a long shot. But gradually, something shifted. The temperature of the home came down. Repair became easier. And most of all, *everyone* — not just the kids — felt less shame. That's what planting a family culture looks like. It's not about being a perfectly peaceful household. It's about creating rhythms, language, and rituals that say *feelings are welcome here, mistakes don't separate us. God is in the room — even in the chaos.* It's okay if the growth is slow. Seeds always look small before they grow into something strong.

From Behaviour Management to Discipleship

It's easy to get caught up in managing behaviour. After all, it's the part we see. It's loud. Disruptive. Public. Behaviour is what other people notice, what schools report on, what strangers judge us for in supermarkets. But behaviour is never the whole story — it's the fruit, not the root. What we're really shaping in these parenting years isn't just polite manners or tidy compliance. It's *the heart* — and not in the moralistic, "just be good" sense. But in the biblical sense: the inner world of belief, emotion, desire, and identity. Jesus didn't come to fix outward behaviour. He came to heal hearts.

So when our parenting focuses only on getting our kids to stop yelling, or follow instructions, or sit quietly in church, we might miss the deeper invitation: to disciple our children — not just discipline them. Discipleship is about teaching our children who they are, whose they are, and how deeply they are loved — especially in the messy moments. It's when we say, "You're not bad — you're having a big feeling. Let's figure it out together." "God still loves you. Nothing you do will change that — and I feel the same." "Let's ask Jesus to help us when we feel out of control."

It's not about being permissive. Boundaries still matter. But our boundaries are held in relationship, not fear. Our correction flows from compassion, not control. We don't want kids who behave well because they're scared of us. We want kids who learn, slowly and surely, that when they fail — they're still safe, still seen, and still loved. Because *that* is the gospel. And when we model it, not just teach it, it becomes the soil their whole emotional and spiritual life can grow from.

Parent Reflection

Take a moment to reflect on what you've planted in your child's heart this week — even if it didn't feel like much.

Maybe you made space for a meltdown instead of rushing to fix it.

Maybe you sat quietly beside a worried child when you didn't have the answers. Maybe you apologised for raising your voice. Maybe you whispered a prayer through tired tears, asking God to fill in the gaps.

You're doing more than you think. Emotional and spiritual formation don't happen in grand gestures. They happen in hallway conversations, school run car rides, whispered prayers at bedtime, and deep breaths taken in the middle of chaos. So often, you won't see the growth straight away. But the soil is being tilled. The roots are going deep. And the seeds you're sowing now will bear fruit in seasons to come.

A Word Over You, Faithful Parent

You don't have to raise fearless children. You don't have to have all the answers. You don't have to be the perfect picture of peace. You just have to show up. Stay close. Keep planting. There will be days when you're weary. When nothing works. When your prayers feel unanswered, and your efforts invisible.

But God sees.

He sees every gentle word you choose, every tantrum you ride out with patience, every moment you hold space for emotions that are still too big for little hearts. He sees you loving like He loves — with grace, with presence and the kind of compassion that changes everything. So take heart, that the work you are doing matters — eternally. Because when you nurture a child's emotional world *with faith*, you're not just shaping behaviour — you're shaping how they see God. And friend, there's no greater legacy than that.

Scripture Index

(A-Z by book, for easy reference)

Scripture	Reference Context
Deuteronomy 6:7	Teaching faith in daily rhythms
Exodus 2:3–10	Jochebed releasing Moses in trust
Isaiah 41:10	God's presence in fear
Isaiah 40:11	God as a gentle shepherd of parents
Jeremiah 1:5	God's intentional design of each child
Matthew 6:34	Anxiety and daily trust

Matthew 11:28–30	Finding rest in Jesus
Luke 2:48–52	Mary and Jesus in the temple
John 11:35	Jesus expressing emotion (grief)
John 16:33	Jesus acknowledging trouble in the world
Romans 5:3–5	Suffering producing perseverance and hope
Romans 12:2	The renewing of the mind
Philippians 4:6–7	Prayer and peace in anxiety
2 Timothy 1:7	Spirit of power, love, and sound mind

Hebrews 4:15	Jesus understands our weaknesses
1 Peter 5:7	Casting our cares on God
Psalm 23	God's comforting presence through hard things
Psalm 34:18	God is close to the brokenhearted
Psalm 56:3	Trusting God when afraid
Psalm 139:13–14	Fearfully and wonderfully made

Topical Index

(Selected themes and where to find them)

Topic	Chapters
Anxiety in Children	1, 2, 3, 4, 5, 6, 7, 9
Avoidance Cycle	3, 5 (includes infographic)
Bedtime & Nighttime Fears	4, 5
Big Feelings / Emotional Expression	2, 4, 6
Body-Based Symptoms (Somatic)	7
Brain Science Made Simple	2, 3, 7

Christian Parenting & Discipleship	1, 5, 8, 11
Co-Regulation Techniques	3, 7 (includes infographic)
Control vs Surrender	8
Devotional Prayers	End of each chapter
Emotional Safety at Home	3, 4, 11
Exposure Ladders	5 (includes ladder graphic)
Faith + Brain Notes	Throughout
Gratitude & Joy Practices	7
Health Anxiety in Parents	8 (personal reflections)

Meltdowns & Behavioural Outbursts	3, 4, 6
Perfectionism in Kids	6
Prayer in Parenting	Throughout, especially 5, 9, 11
Resilience Building	5, 10, 11
Sleepovers & Social Independence	9
Spiritual Formation of Children	1, 5, 11
Tantrums vs Fear Responses	4, 6
Therapeutic Tools at Home	3, 5, 7

Trusting God with Your Child   1, 8, 11

Worry & "What if" Thinking   1, 5

About the Publisher

Erinnah Group Ltd is a registered Charity in Australia equipping families, educators, and churches to raise children who are both emotionally resilient and spiritually anchored. Whether it's through podcasts, school programs, or animated storytelling, our heart is to remind families that God is present in the messiest, most beautiful parts of parenting — and that anxious kids can grow into courageous ones.

Kelly Whittaker, Founding Director of Erinnah Group, is a Christian mental health clinician, writer, producer, and creator of *Erinnah's Treehouse* — the world's first Christian-informed, animated anxiety program designed for children.

With a background in Psychological Science and a Master's in Social Work, Kelly has spent more than a decade helping families navigate emotional and behavioural challenges with clinical wisdom and deep compassion. She is also the founder of the Institute of Sensitive Sleep Consulting, which has trained hundreds of professionals in attachment-informed sleep support.

Kelly blends science and Scripture with warmth, honesty, and a touch of humour — knowing firsthand what it means to be both a clinician and a mum, showing up on the hard days with prayer and caramilk chocolate.

She lives in rural Queensland with her husband Graham (Co-Director, Erinnah Group) and two talented children, where her life is fuelled by Jesus, early mornings, and an ever-growing collection of half-drunk cups of water on the bench.

www.ingramcontent.com/pod-product-compliance
Lightning Source LLC
Chambersburg PA
CBHW072000070526
44583CB00015B/1265